Common Sense

We Are the Guardians of Democracy

Jeff Marsico

Wolf Moon Publishing Company

Elizabethtown, Pennsylvania

Edited by Joshua Rivedal

First Wolf Moon Publishing Company trade paperback edition

December 2024.

For information about special discounts for bulk purchases, speaking engagements, or appearances, contact Wolf Moon Publishing Company (e-mail address above).

ISBN: 978-0-9826938-4-1 (paperback)

ISBN: 978-0-9826938-5-8 (ebook)

About the Author

Jeff Marsico is an average Joe. He grew up in Scranton, Pennsylvania. Went to high school at a public school where he met his wife and they have been married since 1987. Went to college and worked the entire time so he could pay for it, including taking courses on ships while in the Navy, such as Public Speaking where he gave speeches in a Spruance-class destroyer's fan room. He has two children, now thriving adults, and two grandchildren at publication although he hopes for more.

He has no political experience. He did not formally study politics or most other positions he has staked in this book.

Professionally, Jeff is a community bank consultant. Not a Wells Fargo or Bank of America consultant, but an advisor to the banks that make a difference from Anytown USA's Main Street. He, along with his colleagues, started the consultancy, The Kafafian Group, in 2001.

He is also the author of *Squared Away-How Can Bankers Succeed as Economic First Responders*. He serves on the faculty of various state banking associations' executive development programs and is a frequent banking industry speaker and commentator.

Jeff served seven years as a cryptologist in the U.S. Navy, earning three Navy Achievement Medals, the Kuwait Liberation Medal, Southwest Asia Service Medal, Combat Action Ribbon, Sea Service Ribbon, and other commendations.

He is a graduate of the University of Hawaii and has an MBA from Lebanon Valley College.

Table of Contents

Welcome to Common Sense

Sixty-three percent of Americans have little or no confidence in the United States political system[1]. Things need to change—but change has to start with us. If our democracy is to thrive, we must be its guardians.

At no time in history have we had such a wealth of information at our fingertips to have informed opinions. Yet when I hear or read opinions on television, in the news, or on social media, it appears that we don't avail ourselves of it. Why form an opinion on an important issue without first researching it?

One reason is we rely on our news outlets to do the research and inform us. Which news outlet? In my estimation and common-sense observation, the state of our news industry is worse than at any time in my life. No more Walter Cronkite reading the news with little editorial bias, telling us, "That's the way it is." Now, it feels more like, "The way it is according to our incredibly biased editorial staff."

I wrote these chapters to inform you on how I arrived at my opinions on important, even divisive issues of the day. You may not agree with me on some of them or even most of them. But I hope you see that I arrived at my positions because I researched them thoroughly. I have an informed opinion.

Having an informed electorate scares many politicians. In so many cases, they rely on your ignorance to fool you into believing that they are your only hope to avoid the catastrophe of a competing politician. So often, the best policies for achieving what you believe to be government's proper and effective role do not fit into a sound bite. Sound bites favor shallow, ineffective policies that don't survive investigation, common sense, or even the next election cycle.

One of my favorite presidents was Calvin Coolidge, who rose to office upon Warren Harding's sudden death in 1923. He was known as The Great Refrainer because he believed in limited government. He balanced the federal budget every year in office, and federal expenditures were less when he left office in 1929 than when he assumed it.

The United States experienced tremendous prosperity during his tenure. He was so popular he would have been a shoo-in for re-election in 1928, but he chose not to run because it would've made him a 10-year president, and he thought that too long. Imagine!

Yet despite such success as president, the 2024 Presidential Greatness Project Expert Survey ranked him as 34th best out of 45. As it turns out, those surveyed to arrive at this inexplicable ranking of Coolidge between Chester Arthur and Richard Nixon were mostly from the American Political Science Association., an organization that one member cited as only ten percent Republican.[2] Coolidge was a Republican.

If I didn't research it, I would have thought that Coolidge was ineffective. Someone who presided over a 22% increase in GDP, increases in everyone's standard of living, and balanced every budget. Ineffective. If that's ineffective, give me more ineffective.

Although there is much information at our fingertips, we must discern the source of the information we are consuming. Like I had to research the American Political Science Association because common sense told me something was up with their opinion of Coolidge. I dedicated an essay in this book regarding journalism. I suggest a critical look at the bias of whatever you are consuming to arrive at your informed, common-sense position.

The Vital Role of Common Sense in Navigating Contemporary Issues

In an era dominated by rapid technological advancements, information overload, and polarized opinions, common sense has never been more essential. As we face an array of complex and often contentious issues—from climate change and economic disparities to public health and politics—common sense serves as a critical tool for discerning the best course of action. It anchors us in reality, helping to navigate the flood of data and opinions, and ensures that our decisions are not just informed but also practical and grounded in everyday wisdom.

Understanding Common Sense

Common sense is often described as sound judgment derived from experience rather than specialized knowledge. It is the instinctive ability to perceive, understand, and judge things that are shared by nearly all people and can be reasonably expected of nearly all people without the need for debate. While it might seem simplistic, common sense is a powerful and often underestimated form of reasoning that bridges the gap between abstract thinking and practical application. However, common sense alone should not form our opinions on important issues of the day. We must seek and discern knowledge and apply common sense once we acquire knowledge.

The Importance of Common Sense in Decision-Making

Filtering Information: In the digital age, we're bombarded with information from various sources, many of which are biased or misleading. According to Allsides, a media watchdog, almost none of what we consider "mainstream media" earns a "Center" rating.[3] Common sense helps us sift through this information, identify credible sources, and focus on what truly matters. It allows us to cut through the noise and concentrate on the facts that are most relevant to the issue at hand. This is what I did regarding the Presidential Greatness Project.

Preventing Overcomplication: Experts and specialists are invaluable, but sometimes their insights can be overly complex or disconnected from everyday realities. Common sense helps to simplify these complexities, ensuring that decisions are understandable and actionable for the average person. It prevents us from getting lost in the details and helps to maintain focus on practical solutions.

Promoting Balanced Perspectives: In a world where extreme views often dominate discourse, common sense encourages moderation and balance. It prompts us to consider multiple perspectives, weigh the pros and cons, and avoid knee-jerk reactions. This balanced approach is crucial in making decisions that are fair and equitable.

For example, Pennsylvania recently passed its budget, which included funding so schools can provide students with breakfast. I am against it. And my opposition resulted in a heated rebuttal from a social media follower. How could I be against feeding children?! If the follower wanted my logic, which he didn't because he "blocked" me, he would have learned that I don't think a taxpayer who fed their own children should now be compelled to feed other people's children. If having student breakfast is so important, perhaps instead of making it compulsory, we should implement school choice. Those who feel free breakfast is important can choose the school that offers it. I'm not against feeding children. I will stipulate that well-nourished children perform better at school. What I am for is that parents are responsible for feeding their children. Is that an extreme view?

Ensuring Accountability: Common sense fosters a sense of responsibility and accountability. It reminds us that decisions should be made not only based on theoretical outcomes but also on their real-world implications.

Challenges to Common Sense

Despite its importance, common sense is not infallible. It can be clouded by personal biases, cultural differences, and emotional reactions such as from my social media follower. Moreover, in a world where expertise is increasingly specialized, common sense alone may not always provide the full picture. This is why common sense should complement, not replace, expert knowledge. Unbiased expert knowledge. The key is to strike a balance where common sense guides the application of specialized knowledge in a way that is practical and accessible.

Putting it All Together

Common sense is an indispensable tool in navigating the important issues of our time. It serves as a compass, guiding us through the complexities of modern life and ensuring that our decisions are grounded in reality and practicality. While it is not a substitute for unbiased expert knowledge, it provides a necessary counterbalance, helping us make decisions that are not only informed but also reasonable and effective.

In a world that often prioritizes complexity and specialization, common sense reminds us of the value of simplicity and the wisdom of everyday experience. Most reading these words want less poverty, less racism, and more economic mobility. Agree on this, and then it comes down to how to achieve it. Differences of opinion in this context can be accomplished in debate, using expert knowledge and common sense.

I applied common sense to arrive at my opinions in the chapters that follow. My hope is you will do the same. An informed electorate is critical to the success of our democratic republic. Many of our leaders think we are ignorant. Let's prove them wrong.

On Accountability

In 1989, I arrived at my first U.S. Navy duty station in Rota, Spain. I was a kid from Scranton, Pennsylvania, who had hardly left my hometown. To get on a plane and fly across the Atlantic Ocean to a different country was sensory overload. You would think that with so many new experiences, none would stand out.

But one did and has been seared in my memory ever since. My division officer, Lieutenant Junior Grade Proper called all newly arriving sailors into his office to brief us on the culture he was trying to create. When my turn came, he told me to avoid pointing fingers because the other three would be pointing back at me. I have no idea what else he said. But I remember what he told me about being accountable. Own your situation.

Fast forward to today, and personal accountability is hard to come by. We rarely see it from politicians. Recently, both former President Trump and President Biden were involved in imbroglios regarding mishandling classified documents. Trump had them in his basement and Biden had them in an office and his garage.

Trump's response, "President Barack Hussein Obama kept 33 million pages of documents, much of them classified."[4] In other words, "Oh yeah! He did it too!" Diffusing responsibility for what he had done based on what others have done. That's not personal accountability, that's relative accountability; as if President Obama bore any responsibility for President Trump's actions.

President Biden, not to be outdone in deflecting accountability for having classified documents in his garage, said, "As I said earlier this week, and by the way, my Corvette is in a locked garage, so it's not like they're sitting out on the street."[5] His deflection revolved around not knowing he had classified documents and that they were locked up with his Corvette anyway. He claimed ignorance so he didn't have to be accountable.

By way of comparison, while I was in the Navy, a shipmate accidentally took a few pages of classified material out of our secure facility. When he realized what he had done, he destroyed the documents and self-reported to his supervisor. He was demoted in rank. He took ownership of his situation and suffered the consequences.

Conversely, top government officials have had no such inclination to take ownership of their situation. They likely will receive no consequences for their actions or their subsequent lack of personal accountability.

When my daughter was in high school, a few of her friends were caught drinking at a dance. The teacher chaperone asked my daughter's friend, who was accompanying the intoxicated girl if she was drinking. She confessed and was suspended from the soccer team just as playoffs were about to begin.

Had she lied and deflected any accountability, she probably would not have been suspended because there would have been no way for the chaperone teacher to know if she was lying unless her other friends owned up to it. Her father was angry that the teacher asked her without him being there. As if that would've led to her deflecting ownership of the situation. She probably would have avoided the soccer suspension. But at what cost?

Here's another story from our unaccountable culture. A morning television show was running a news segment on the growing debt in school lunch programs. They paraded expert after expert on camera to entice the federal government into doing something about it.

When I went to school, my mother sent my brothers and me to school every day with brown bag lunches. My father passed away when I was young, so we lived off my mom's clerical job and the Social Security survivor's fund available for child survivors of Social Security participants. In other words, we didn't have a lot of money. But my mom never off-loaded her responsibility to feed her children onto the school district. Parents should be accountable for feeding their children, not the government, schools, or "society."

Why don't parents take accountability for their children?

That's where we are in society. Better to deflect or offload accountability than to own it.

It's not always this way. Sports is a highly accountable profession, with talking heads commenting on your performance in real-time with stats aplenty. Trevor Lawrence, an NFL quarterback, after throwing four interceptions in the first half of a playoff game that resulted in a 27-0 deficit, said this of his performance, "Definitely the worst half of my football life." He owned it.

The team bounced back to win that game, and Lawrence went on to say, "Those guys beside me and the ones on the other side of the ball (defense) never lost faith in me. That's one thing that makes it easier when you got guys that believe in you no matter what the circumstances are." He owned the mistakes of the first half and dispensed credit for the comeback to his teammates.

And perhaps owning the first half led to the adjustments needed to come back in the second half. If all Lawrence did, even if just in his mind rather than behind a microphone, was point fingers and blame a poor running game or receivers running bad routes, then he would have to make no adjustments. It's not his fault, it's theirs. Likely outcome, no comeback. Accountability matters.

In far more instances, however, we lack accountability. We are not owning our situations. We don't reflect on what we could have done better if we experienced a negative result. There are people around us—leaders, family, and friends—who may be well-meaning but quick to soothe our egos by telling us it's not our fault. It's someone else's, and sometimes someone else is some non-existent or barely existent but fully conjured boogeyman. And we accept it. Because it's easier to point the finger, rather than recognize the three pointing back at us.

How does this play out in society?

Let's take something that is all too common in the news. A teenager gets shot after an argument after school. The person who should be accountable: the shooter. What transpires? The news blames guns, society, anything but the person who should own it, the shooter. In a totally accountable society, I would handicap the shooter as 90%+ responsible, maybe 8% parents, and the crumbs that are left could be at the feet of society or some other boogeyman. Yet all we talk about is the 2%. Wouldn't it be better to focus on the 90%? Or, in the case of a minor, the 8%, too?

In addition, no one is asking the victim to reflect on how that situation could've been avoided. That would be "victim blaming." No asking, "What could I have done differently?" so the victim didn't end up in that situation. Had the victim been accountable, there would be a greater likelihood he would avoid such situations in the future. But in today's no-accountability culture, that self-reflection wouldn't happen.

Even suggesting the victim reflect and hold themselves accountable for being in that situation could bring whoever suggested it a world of scrutiny (i.e., "victim blaming"). Since the actions, environment, and emotions that led to the shooting were not the fault of the victim, then no modifications are required. It's the shooter's, guns, and society's fault. And it is much more likely to repeat itself.

In the above example, there is little mention of the parents' accountability. Isn't it the parents' responsibility to send well-behaved, law-abiding, teacher-respecting children to school ready to learn? Today, if a teacher disciplines a child, the parent often blames the teacher or school. Not so when I was a child. If I got in trouble, my mom put me in a world of hurt. In today's no-personal-accountability culture, that's less likely the case.

More alarming than not holding ourselves personally accountable is society's attempt to absolve people of the consequences of their actions. A case in point is the federal government's attempt to "forgive" student loans for those who recently borrowed to go to college. There is no wiping away that debt. If we tell someone they don't have to pay it, we have to tell someone else to pay it. It's a transfer of responsibility. It's a transfer of accountability.

So, if a recent graduate chose a more expensive school, a low-paying or unmarketable profession, or simply did the six-year plan with a couple of overseas semesters, are we doing them favors by absolving them of the consequences of their decisions?

What about the student who went to state school and worked to defray their college costs and, therefore, have minimal to no student loans? Is it fair to make them accountable for paying for the other student's two semesters in London?

How about the parents who sacrificed and saved for their child's college, buying used cars and living in a smaller house so their children didn't have student loans? Do we now ask them to pay for the parents who always had the nicest cars, biggest houses, and went on the cool vacations but didn't have money for their children's college?

What are we telling those students and their parents about accountability? It would be better if we made the parent pull up to their neighbor's house in their Lexus, knock on their door, and ask them, "Hey, could you pay for my kid's college? And, oh, by the way, nice Chevy." At least there would be some consequence and some ownership of their situation, rather than offloading accountability from their decisions onto someone else that they never have to stare in the face.

If we had a highly accountable culture, prior to college (or technical school) the parents would sit with the student at the kitchen table, evaluate schools and tuition, compare to what the family has saved, determine how much needs to be borrowed, what those payments would be when they are due, and the average compensation of the profession the student is studying for.

The parents are accountable to their children as parents, advisors, and mentors. The student is accountable for their decisions and the consequences of those decisions. A more informed decision would likely be made. And the parent wouldn't be knocking on the neighbor's door to pay for what transpired that evening at the family kitchen table—they wouldn't even consider it.

But that is not where we are today. Should it be?

On Education

My school district has 3,700 students. From the 2017-18 school year to the 2021-22 school year, the cost per student escalated from $16,500 to $18,800, and it has been rising consistently. Why?

When I put this question to the district's communications director, he gave me two reasons: 1) unfunded state mandates, and 2) charter schools. According to the district, a student who selects a charter school drains approximately $12,000 from the district's coffers without the district's expenses going down commensurately.

And if the charter school, mainly a cyber charter school being utilized by home-schooling parents, costs $7,000 per student less than the district can deliver, perhaps we should want more to attend charter schools.

When I asked a school board member about the escalating cost per student, he was unaware of the number, saying the district's numbers were different. All I did was take the annual budget and divide it by the number of students. He responded that they don't count debt service in the cost per student. But don't taxpayers pay the debt service?

The school board member considered himself conservative and assured me the district was not wasting taxpayer money. It would be surprising if anyone involved in the education bureaucracy would admit to wasting taxpayer money. Let's say I'm skeptical, as we all should be.

The cost of $18,800 per student equates to $470,000 per class (if a class has 25 students). Teachers, we often hear, make meager wages. According to teacher.org's review of Bureau of Economic Analysis data, the average teacher's salary was $61,820 in 2022. That sounds reasonable, and one might consider it a little low. Although you probably have to annualize that salary based on the 10-month work schedule, increasing that apples-to-apples comparison to other professions to $74,185. But wait, there's more! According to the same source, teacher benefits add 45% as part of that total compensation number.[6] Compare that to 19-25%, which is more typical for private employees.

So, teacher total compensation for our hypothetical $470,000 classroom would absorb approximately $90,000 of it, on average. Where does the other $380,000 go? Obviously, the cost doesn't reside solely in the classroom. According to the National Center for Education Statistics (NCES), in the 2020-21 school year, schools spent 6.6% on administration, 8.0% on operations and maintenance, and 19.3% on "other school services," adding another $159,330 per year for our hypothetical class.[7] That brings our total number including the teacher to approximately $250,000—slightly over half of what the cost is.

My local high school has about 1,200 of the total district's 3,700 students. That is about 48 classes if divided by 25 students per class. At 33.9% of the $470,000 per class, that equates to approximately $7.6 million for administration, operations and maintenance, and "other school services." Seems reasonable.

But it's not. According to the Brookings Institute, half of a school district's personnel are not teachers. [8] These can include librarians (or library media specialists), English as a Second Language or bilingual teacher aides, special education instructional aides, and a variety of other instructional aides that also work directly with students. Among administrative staff, schools have principals, but they also have vice or assistant principals, secretaries and other clerical support staff, instructional coordinators and supervisors such as curriculum specialists, and a variety of non-instructional aides. Schools also employ health services staff such as school or guidance counselors, nurses, social workers, psychologists, and speech therapists; and they employ basic services staff such as food service personnel, custodial, maintenance and security personnel, and special education non-instructional aides.

So, in addition to adding the cost of $159,330 for administration, operations and maintenance, and "other school services," we have to include another $90,000 to account for the 1:1 teacher-to-non-teacher ratio. So now, our math changes to: $90,000 for the teacher, $159,330 for administration, operations and maintenance, and "other school services," we add another $90,000. Grand total: $340,000. Still nearly $130,000 less than the taxes and fees collected per class.

Where does it go?

Should we concede the 1-1 ratio? When I went to high school, our entire grade had one guidance counselor. I think there may have been two or three janitors. According to a 2014 study by the Thomas Fordham Institute, the number of non-teaching staff in the United States (those employed by school systems but not serving as classroom teachers) grew by 130 percent between 1970-2010.[9] Key findings of that study include:

- Since 1950, school staffing has increased by nearly 400 percent, and non-teaching personnel have played a major part in that growth.
- The United States spends far more on non-teaching staff (as a percentage of education spending) than most of our economic peers in the OECD (Organization for Economic Co-operation and Development).
- Over the last forty years, the biggest driver of growth in non-teachers has been in the teacher-aide category.
- School districts vary greatly relative to their number of employed personnel, but those differences likely stem from staffing decisions made by leaders.

My school district's communications director would cite unfunded mandates, such as a state requirement that a school district have a speech therapist for every "x-amount" of students in the district. It is easy for state legislators to mandate costs to school districts. State taxes don't have to go up, yet it appears on the state representative's resumé as something good they accomplished. Schools, however, mostly through real estate taxes, have to pass that cost on to their district's residents. The state rep is the hero—the school board is the villain.

Schools, however, are significantly funded by state grants. So, one way to bring discipline to state legislators telling schools what to do is to assess the cost of what is proposed and increase the state grant to the school districts to cover the cost. Secondarily, when state legislators propose school districts do something different and incur costs to do it, the purpose of the mandate should be clear and there should be some test to determine if the goal was achieved. If the goal is not achieved, the mandate automatically sunsets. It makes little sense for a proposal to be enacted, doesn't work, and the school keeps doing it and taxpayers keep paying for it.

To bridge the gap, where we lack accountability for the effectiveness of funded or unfunded mandates, to more accountability, why don't we have a non-partisan study of mandates imposed and their effectiveness? Each mandate has a constituent. So, there will be someone at the school board meeting or at the state budget hearing lobbying to keep their mandate because of "the children." However, the continued escalation of the cost of education in our country and the repeated pleas for more money has to stop. Our schools haven't gotten better because of it.

More than 20 years ago, I was on my church's finance council. As part of our duties, we helped manage our elementary school budget. At that time, we charged $2,500 for tuition. Our grades were K-5. Each class had between 10-20 children. The school was heavily subsidized by the Sunday collection plate, and we ultimately had to close it.

Prior to public education, churches educated children—primarily the Catholic church. Moving from illiterate to enlightened was largely due to the church. Today, church schools are in retreat because of the reasons we had to close our school.

But it wouldn't have to be that way if tuition costs to private schools were not on top of what we pay in taxes to support public schools. Meaning, if you want to send your child to a private school, there is no discount on your taxes (state or local) because you are not using public schools. So, only the most affluent get to send their kids to private schools… or the most impoverished who can get most of their private school tuition paid for.

This is how it played out for me. My father died of cancer when I was six. On his deathbed, he asked my mother to keep us three boys in Catholic school for as long as possible. He knew we would be at risk of turning out badly without a father. My mother kept her promise, keeping us in private school until eighth grade with the generous support of parishioners of St. Clare's and St. Paul's churches. Not everyone gets that chance.

According to the most recent National Assessment of Educational Progress (NAEP), private school students score better on standardized tests in almost all subjects.[10] Supporters of public schools say this is because of background differences between private versus public school students (e.g., learning abilities, single parent vs. two parents in the home, socioeconomic status, etc.). Private school supporters cite smaller class sizes and student academic performance as reasons why private schools are better.

Regardless of which one you support, based on how we fund education, the choice is only available to those parents who can afford the additional tuition of the private school or the impoverished who would likely receive support like my family did. Moderate- to middle-income families have no such choice.

Why do we do this? The commonsense reason is that if a school district implements school choice and provides vouchers for private schools, then parents who are actively involved in their child's education will likely go to private schools. Those who are not will keep their children in whatever school is most convenient. This would likely decrease the quality of education in the public schools based on adverse selection and would drain public schools of their money supply.

So, we choose to keep the children trapped in what is often an inferior learning environment, stunting their eventual economic mobility. Anti-voucher advocates won't say what you just read because the reality does not support "the children." One reason for the growing disparity between the haves and the have-nots is education. And those that exhort "privilege" mean, in part, that higher-income families can afford to send their children to better schools while lower-income families can't. It is a peculiar hill for anti-choice adults to die on.

We try to avoid this reality of creating a greater divide between the privileged who can attend private schools and those who can't by passing legislation to try to help public schools get better. By storming school board meetings parents can influence curriculum so administrators, having a government-sponsored monopoly and being mostly from one ideological bent, can't recruit our children to their way of thinking. We throw money at public education—gobs and gobs of money—and the schools keep asking for more.

Why not support school choice?

School choice will create competition. Choice gives parents the power to put their children in schools consistent with their values so they don't have to storm school board meetings to challenge what dogma is being taught to their children. If the parent had the choice to pick schools for their children, the power would shift from school boards, unions, and school administrators to them. Choice gives parents the power to fire failing schools, providing plenty of motivation for schools not to fail.

If public schools are so good, and some would argue they're superior to private schools, why worry about parents having the choice of where to send their children to school? I mentioned in the introduction that I opposed free breakfasts at school because we are offloading the responsibility to feed children from parents to taxpayers. But if free breakfasts are important to parents, they can select the school that offers it. If it's so important to all parents, then all competing schools would offer it. In this scenario, what I think about free breakfast is far less important than what the parent thinks. Isn't this how it should be?

Choice would require a transition from our current system. School districts can't afford to lose 50% of their funding overnight. They would have to prepare to operate on a lower budget, with fewer students and therefore fewer staff and property and grounds.

This wouldn't be an overnight situation because we are structured for the education monopoly. We are culturally acclimated to it. Legislators are used to passing laws and regulating to improve schools rather than encouraging competition to make them better. There are unions vehemently opposed to choice because teachers will be judged on quality rather than tenure. Bad teachers will be dismissed. Great teachers would garner greater pay than average teachers. And there is an entire education bureaucracy that has led to a teacher to non-teacher 1-1 ratio.

Why not give parents the choice to send their children to the best schools for them? They are most qualified to make that choice.

College

For generations, we have been told that education is the greatest fuel for upward mobility. We have also been told that college is the ticket. And there is merit to it. In 2021, full-time workers ages 22 to 27 who held a bachelor's degree but had no further education made a median annual wage of $52,000, compared with $30,000 for full-time workers of the same age with a high school diploma and no degree, according to data from the Bureau of Labor Statistics.[11]

However, in the Pew Research study cited above, only 62% of those who enter college graduate within six years—meaning we have a lot of dropouts who likely pay very high tuition and end up with little benefit. Rather than going to college, it would be better if they went to trade school, the military, or directly into the workforce.

But that would deny colleges that one or two years of tuition. And college costs have been soaring. Like primary and secondary education, colleges backed up the truck on their bureaucracy. In 2021, college instructional spending represented only 27.4% of total spending, while spending on academic support, student services, and institutional support was 22.9%.[12] College has been a great deal for college administrators. And less so for students, particularly the 38% who do not walk away with a college degree within six years.

In reviewing the 20 most in-demand jobs for 2023 published by AARP, half require either no degree or a technical degree.[13] Why do we push so many of our kids to college when it is not without risk? Sure, those who finish college with marketable degrees will likely out-earn those who do not throughout their lifetime. College is a bad deal for those who are pushed into it when it does not suit them and then drop out. It's surely a bad deal for those who major in degrees with no clear path to employment. An expensively bad deal.

The challenge is to identify one student from the other. Here is where parents should be accountable. When determining their high school student's next step, they have to assess if college is right for them, what will be the in-demand professions upon graduation, and what schools are best for their children. It's important work and should not be outsourced to an administrator whose agenda might be different, even contrary, to the parents and/or students.

Students are also accountable for their future. What a great lesson for them to learn instead of being taught that every obstacle they've encountered so far was not their fault. They have to start owning their decisions. And if they want to be a chef, then after going through the finances, education, and apprenticeship needed to succeed, you send them on their way. Pushing them off to college for a party year and then dropping out only benefits the college that got that one year of tuition.

One last thing about post-secondary education. As a society, we should grant scholarships first and foremost for the professions most in demand and secondarily for need. If we are expending public money, be it federal, state, or even not-for-profit, we owe it to taxpayers and/or givers to direct those dollars towards professions that do the most public good, in terms of tax dollars, or consistent with a charity's objectives, if from a charity. If we anticipate having a long-term shortage of truck drivers, shouldn't our money be directed to developing more truck drivers? Common sense.

On Capitalism

I took five economics classes in college but not by choice. I transferred schools and was required to take five even though I was not an economics major. I remember all five economics professors. Three of them were immigrants, two of which were refugees from Vietnam and Iran and the other was from Pakistan—three countries I would not herald as pillars of economic success.

All three professors were unapologetic capitalists. But they hailed from countries that are either heavily government-controlled, socialist, or theocratic. Why support capitalism? Perhaps it was precisely because they experienced centrally controlled economies. And they were in a position to predict the outcome; greater poverty and lower economic mobility. So, they left. You won't find Americans knocking down doors to get into Iran, Pakistan, or Vietnam.

Remember East Germany? The communists had to build a wall to stop East Germans from trying to escape to West Germany, a capitalist economy. I encourage you to look at a nighttime satellite photo of the Korean peninsula for a stark visual of a centrally controlled versus a capitalist economy.

This essay should stop here. Case made. Human striving shows over and over people fleeing centrally controlled economies to freer ones. Yet here we are, having to make a case that has already been made.

Edward P. Lazar, in his 2017 research *Socialism, Capitalism, and Income,*[14] concluded the following:

> *"The general evidence suggests that both across countries and over time within a country, providing more economic freedom improves the incomes of all groups, including the lowest group. As countries liberalize their economic environment, incomes, including those of the lowest decile, grow."*

Most critics of capitalism generally don't advocate an about-face to socialism. The evidence is too aligned against it. The United States has a somewhat mixed economy, with approximately 20-23% of gross domestic product a result of government spending. I should note that taxes represent 17-20% of GDP, hence the U.S.'s persistent government deficits. The main argument for those espousing more government control is the disparities in income and wealth distribution in a freer economy.

Although the evidence supports that everyone is better off in a freer economy, some are far better off than others. This is to be expected. In fact, in a socialist economy, where the government exercises significant control over the economy, government bureaucrats do quite well, as do those who find favor from those bureaucrats. Neither Vladimir Putin nor his buddy oligarchs are struggling to pay their mortgages.

The wealth distribution in a socialist society is highly concentrated, but not to those who take risks, invest their capital, suffer losses, and reap the rewards of the decisions they've made and the risks they've taken. In socialism, it is those with the fingers on the pulse of government that benefit most. Disparity in income and wealth is not the sole domain of capitalism. In socialism, economic power is more concentrated in the hands of very few. Personal economic mobility is more a result of who you know, rather than what you know or what you do.

There is no denying income and wealth are not distributed evenly in a capitalist society. Should it? Should Bill Gates be fabulously rewarded, as he has been, by coming up with a business model in high demand, having dedicated countless hours and resources to making it happen, and then having the resulting business take off? Should we expect his income and wealth to be greater than, say another Microsoft employee who might have joined the company Gates created, took little risk in doing so, and makes a good living at Microsoft but is nothing like what Gates makes or is worth?

If we forced Gates to close that gap and make the same as those employees, what would be his motivation to take that risk, invest those resources, and create a company that currently employs over 200,000? Although that Microsoft employee likely makes a good, living wage, and is better off than if Gates hadn't created the company, there is a very large wealth and income gap between the two.

This doesn't sound like an opportunity problem, or a standard of living problem, or a wage growth problem. It sounds like an envy problem.

Charlie Munger, the former Warren Buffet partner at Berkshire Hathaway, was in his 90s and already wealthy when he said this about envy:

> *If you take the last 100 years (1922-2022) most of modernity came in that last 100 years. In the previous 100 years, we got another chunk of modernity. Before that, life was pretty brutal, short and limited. It's amazing how much achievement that occurred in civilization in the last 100 years. In spite of all of this enormous increase in living standards, people are less happy with the state of affairs than when things were much tougher. And that has a very simple explanation: the world is not driven by greed, it's*

> *driven by envy. The fact that everybody is five times better off than they used to be, they take it for granted. All that they think about is that somebody else has more and it's not fair that they should have it and they don't. It's weird for somebody my age. In the middle of the great depression when the hardship was unbelievable, I felt safer walking around Omaha in the evening than walking around my neighborhood in Los Angeles after all of this great wealth and so forth. Other people are driven crazy by it [envy]. And other people play to envy to advance their own political careers. We have whole networks now that pour gasoline on the flames of envy. I like the religion of the old Jews. The people that were against envy. Not the people that profit from it.*[15]

Is our country and the world better off for having Bill Gates create Microsoft? It's a rhetorical question. And the answer goes further than those who benefit from Microsoft's existence. Gates and his ex-wife started a foundation where they are systematically funding projects around the world to make the world better, doing so via vaccinations to end disease and with freshwater projects in poor countries.

But capitalism isn't all sunshine and rainbows.

Crony Capitalism

The most significant black eye to capitalism is crony capitalism, a pejorative term describing how participants in an economy seek favor from governments to either keep competitors out, garner subsidies or tax breaks, or influence laws or regulations favorable to them. If there were no crony capitalists, would we have so many government lobbyists?

All lobbying is not bad lobbying—particularly when the result is to keep government from excessively regulating an industry. However, lobbying to court government favor through subsidies, tax breaks or preferential contracts, differing regulatory rule applications, or simply protecting "cronies" from competition is bad for free markets, players within the marketplace, economic growth, and the efficient allocation of capital.

There are times when governments can intervene in the free market to meet a goal that the free market might not be prepared to undertake on its own. This, however, should be limited to those initiatives that are for the public good yet might take too long to come to fruition if the free market were left to decide. An example is the march toward clean energy. Compared to coal, oil, and gas, it is simply too expensive for consumers. So, the government has stepped in to provide subsidies for things such as solar and wind energy and electric vehicles that currently cost materially more than gas-powered vehicles.

These subsidies should have a dollar and time limit. If the goal of the subsidy has not been met over a reasonable time, they should automatically and without further action sunset. Eventually, there will be plenty of lobbyists from the solar industry roaming the halls of Congress to keep these subsidies in place to protect their interests. If we tried something for the public good and it didn't work, extending these subsidies would be defined as crony capitalism. The solar industry would be using government favor to beat its marketplace competition: other energy suppliers making it without favor because consumers chose them.

Other examples of crony capitalism:

- Government bailouts of corporations during stress events.
- Awarding government contracts to politically favored people or connected companies.

- Bribery and kickbacks to government bureaucrats to court favor from them.

In order to minimize the impact of crony capitalism, it will be critical for governments to be transparent about issuing favor and why.

Another means to reduce crony capitalism is to have strong anti-corruption laws in place where the risk of getting caught outweighs the benefit gained by influencing government favor. This comes with a twist because businesses already must follow so many laws and regulations that it is difficult to keep up. One back door into gaining government favor is to highlight missteps by the competition so that the full force of the government comes down on the wrongdoer, even if the wrongdoing was minimal or an honest mistake. So, simplifying laws and regulations would serve to reduce the incidents of crony capitalism and make it easier to do business.

Another means to reduce crony capitalism is to promote competition and reduce barriers to entry. A key tactic of crony capitalism is to use the power of government to erect barriers of entry for a competitor. Incumbency already has its benefits for businesses in an industry. Amazon has the resources to out-compete Mom and Pop retail shops in pricing power, marketing, and technology. Why protect them from other retailers? Perhaps if it were done for Sears, we would have no Amazon, and we would still be buying belts at the mall.

This provides a segue into another inefficiency of capitalism: barriers to entry and worker immobility.

Barriers

Abraham Lincoln was a lawyer before becoming a politician. He had a fifth-grade education. Today, to be a lawyer, one must go to college, major in some unnecessary degree such as political science, go to law school, and pass the bar exam in one or more states. I am all for having qualified attorneys. The law is more complex than it was in the 19th century, mostly because we have full-time lawmakers doing nothing but making laws or arguing about making laws. Only rarely do they eliminate laws. The requirements to be a lawyer, or "admitted into the bar," have resulted in hourly fees of $500 or more because we have erected barriers to limit the number of lawyers. If you leaped all the barriers, good for you. You are likely doing very well for yourself. But upon reflection, do these barriers make sense?

In my home state of Pennsylvania, there is a two-tiered certification program for becoming a teacher.[16] The first tier requires the prospective teacher to have a bachelor's degree, complete an approved teacher's education program, intern or student teach for a minimum time period observed by a licensed teacher, and then pass a certification test.

If you pursued a career in biology, worked in a lab for 20 years, and were a member of a biotechnology trade association with appropriate continuing education requirements, you would not be qualified to teach biology in Pennsylvania, and likely in most states. Worse, if you did pursue teacher certifications, you would start at compensation levels similar to recent college graduates with education degrees. You probably wouldn't do it.

And good for teachers—keeping others out of their profession that might serve to drive down wages or the handsome benefits packages they receive. According to USAFacts.org, proficiency in reading has not materially changed in the United States since 2000, and math since 2005.[17] Thirty-one percent of 8th-grade students are proficient in reading, and twenty-six percent are proficient in math. Has erecting barriers to entry for teachers benefited our children?

The over-certification in a capitalist society serves mostly to limit competition for those fields requiring certification. Lobbying government to require these barriers is a form of crony capitalism.

Another barrier that inhibits the efficient means of production within a capitalist economy is restricting the flow of labor. In the chapter "On Health," I discuss de-coupling health care from employment leading to a more fluid workforce, one that doesn't anchor employees to an ill-fitted career to "keep the benefits."

This barrier, however, flows both ways. I work for a small company. We hire slowly because we want to be able to keep those workers sufficiently occupied. But also because we fire even slower. It's not that we are slow to recognize a mismatch in employee attitude, effort, and abilities that would lead us to let them go. It is because there are so many protected classes of employees that we fear letting them go would lead to a distractive and expensive lawsuit.

Many states are now considering including obese employees as a protected class. This would pretty much put all but a select few in protected classes. When an employee is fired, how often do they think walking out the door, "I deserved it"? No. They call an employment attorney who goes through the checklist of protected classes in order to go after the employer for discrimination. Each time my firm had to part ways with an employee, it cost us more than the owed wages. In some cases, much more—just to have them sign a waiver that they would not sue us. This was money that we could not pay the other employees, all because we gave it as a parting gift to the terminated employee. Think of the perverse incentives.

I understand the intention of making obese employees a protected class. Many health care plans increase premiums if employees of an employer have bad health experiences. Obese people tend to have more unhealthy experiences driving up premiums in the company. How to mitigate this risk is discussed in the "On Health" chapter.

But of the one million employment discrimination cases filed with the Equal Employment Opportunity Commission (EEOC) or state and local partner agencies from 2010-18, less than 2% in which these agencies completed an investigation was determined to be discriminatory.[18] For those that discrimination actually occurred, your case is significantly diluted by those who file discrimination lawsuits because they got fired and hired an aggressive attorney.

This perverts capitalism. Not only should capitalism facilitate the free flow of capital from those who have capital to those who need it absent of political influence, it should provide for the free flow of labor. When employers can't fire people or it is prohibitively expensive to do so, they are slower to hire people. When intermediaries such as unions protect mediocre or poor employees from being fired or prevent superior employees from receiving superior compensation for performance, we get what we have in our education system.

Agency

Agency is a wonky term that I was hesitant to use. It means that those who either don't own or are minority owners of something, such as a business, yet exert outsized influence over its operations. For this portion of the chapter, I am referring to executives in any business or entity, such as the CEO of GE or the superintendent of the local school district.

Recently, the United Auto Workers went on strike in the U.S. Their main beef was that their wages were stagnant even though their individual auto companies' CEO's compensation went up four-fold. I do not believe an auto worker should be paid near what the CEO is paid, but it is an incredibly bad look for executive compensation to skyrocket while the compensation of the producers of the automobiles barely budged—and the union called them out on it.

More egregious examples of executives flexing their agency muscles include the $1.2 million office renovation of a Merrill Lynch executive, including a $35,000 toilet seat, immediately prior to Merrill's emergency sale to Bank of America. And who can forget the lavish art, parties, and apartment spending of Tyco's former CEO, which was estimated to be over $600 million?

All this gives capitalism a bad name—and it is generally enabled by a company's board of directors, who are likely executives themselves in their respective companies and who show up on the "compensation study" reports given to boards when setting executive compensation. Are there CEOs and other executives who deserve their compensation based on responsibility and performance? Of course. Are there grifters earning high compensation or other goodies without commensurate performance? Unfortunately, yes.

To mitigate this risk, any executive compensation that is over "x" times the average workers' compensation in that company should be disclosed and should not be tax deductible. That motivates boards to set reasonable compensation and executives to elevate the compensation of rank-and-file employees, who enjoy little agency over the company they work for.

Crony capitalism, barriers, and agency are challenges within a free economy. Even with these challenges, capitalism is the single best system to raise standards of living and provide economic mobility and the freedom to pursue an individual's dreams. If you don't believe me, follow immigration patterns. In 2020, an estimated 281 million migrants left one country for another. The number one country sought by these migrants: The United States of America.[19]

On Elections

In the 2008 presidential primaries, a political action committee (PAC) called Citizens United produced a documentary that was detrimental to candidate Hillary Clinton. However, releasing it would violate the 2002 Campaign Reform Act (also known as the McCain-Feingold Act), which barred corporations and unions from paying for media that mentioned any candidate in periods immediately preceding elections.

Citizens United sought relief from the 2002 Act. In 2010, the Supreme Court took up the case, now known as Citizens United v. Federal Election Commission (FEC). In a 5-4 decision, the Supreme Court held that the free speech clause of the First Amendment prohibits the government from limiting independent expenditures on political campaigns by groups such as corporations and labor unions.

The majority opinion reads:

> *"Although the First Amendment provides that 'Congress shall make no law... abridging the freedom of speech,' 2 U.S.C. §441b's prohibition on corporate independent expenditures is an outright ban on speech, backed by criminal sanctions. It is a ban notwithstanding the fact that a PAC created by a corporation can still speak, for a PAC is a separate association from the corporation. Because speech is an essential mechanism of democracy-it is the means to hold officials accountable to the people-political speech must prevail against laws that would suppress it by design or inadvertence. Laws burdening such speech are subject to strict scrutiny, which requires the Government to prove that the restriction 'furthers a compelling interest and is narrowly tailored to achieve that interest.'"*[20]

Ever since that decision, elections have been heavily influenced by big-money Super PACs that are not restricted in their spending or the donations they take in. Their main restriction is that they cannot consort with individual candidates. However, they can run puff ads for candidates and negative ads against candidates, and they can be for or against certain issues.

Most political ads that don't contain the candidate saying, "I am Jane Doe, and I approved this message," are likely run by PACs or Super PACs. PACs are restricted as to contributions, much like direct contributions to candidates are restricted. So wealthy individuals, corporations, unions, or other associations that pour millions into PACs likely do so via Super PACs.

The Citizens United decision is changing elections in ways unthinkable. For example, in 2022, Maryland was electing a new governor because their then governor, Larry Hogan, reached his term limit. Running for the governor's party ticket was someone from his cabinet, who Hogan endorsed, and a weaker candidate who had promoted conspiracy theories about the 2020 presidential election.

The Democratic Governors Association (DGA) stepped in—to a Republican race—in support of the weaker candidate who had a far less chance of beating the Democrat in the general election.[21] Now we have opposition PACs supporting weak candidates in primaries so the stronger candidates lose.

This is nonsense, and we have ourselves to blame for allowing ads to influence our decision on who to vote for or against.

This isn't to say we should ignore ads that might highlight negative information about a candidate, but at a minimum, it should be researched for its validity. Because creating misinformation from actual facts has risen to an art form.

For example, in the 2022 Pennsylvania Senate general election, the National Republican Senatorial Committee (NRSC) PAC ran an ad against Democratic candidate John Fetterman.

The ad said that Fetterman embraced parts of the Green New Deal that would cost you 50,000 bucks a year. Well, Fetterman did not embrace the Green New Deal, and the 50,000 number is a contrived figure conjured by a think tank assuming all facets and timing of the Green New Deal's implementation. Mind you, Fetterman supports an orderly transition to renewable energy, but over decades, and not the 10-year timeframe targeted in the Green New Deal.

If you wondered where Fetterman stood on climate change, his preferred response to it, and the timing and cost of that response, you better not be relying on the NRSC ads to get that information. And so it goes, on and on, with ads that pick pieces of the truth, often out of context, to trick you into believing something about a candidate that is mostly or wholly untrue. Lies are best told with sprinkles of truth convincingly spoken in darkness.

We should all support free speech. So, if the NCRC or the DGA have something to say about a candidate or issue, there could be some truth to it that merits further investigation. Don't expect the NCRC to highlight negative information about a preferred candidate. But you might hear it from the DGA. Use the billions (yes, billions) spent by PACs on national elections to your advantage.

However, in the end, it is our responsibility to come out of the darkness. Our democracy depends on it.

Make Elections Easier

There is an organization, the League of Women Voters (LWV), that hosted debates and sent questionnaires to candidates to collect their positions on important issues of the office sought. It was a one-stop shop to do candidate research prior to voting so we could vote for those who would best represent us. The problem: the LWV tilted, then wilted to one political viewpoint.

In 1976, during the presidential election, then-Senator Bob Dole commented on the LWV: "They're very fine. But they tend to be a little bit liberal." In 2018, the LWV CEO was arrested for crowding a Senate office building, demanding lawmakers reject a Supreme Court nominee.

In 2022 in Pennsylvania, only 30% of Republican candidates completed LWV's VOTE411.org informational guide for the primaries, compared with 70% of Democrats, according to the League of Women Voters of Pennsylvania.

LWV's standing among Republicans was summed up by Catalina Lauf, a Republican candidate for Congress from Illinois, claiming the league "peddles Marxist ideology" and is "anti-American." "Because their hyper-partisanship is turning off a lot of women who just want common sense."[22] Shouldn't we all want common sense?

Although the LWV's attempt to be a one-stop shop for non-partisan voting information was effective for a period of time, choosing sides makes VOTE411.org ineffective.

The idea, though, is a good one. Have a one-stop shop for candidate information in the form of a digital two-page CV or resumé. Page one would read like a resumé with a less than 50-word intro statement with their past experience, education, etc. The second page would contain less than 50-word answers to the top five questions on voters' minds for the office sought.

If the candidate is running for school board, there would be no questions about inflammatory topics such as abortion because that is not germane to the local school board.

Partisanship could creep into the questions asked and the tone of the question, such as a county commissioner being asked: "Are you for or against voter suppression?" Or whether a question is asked at all. However, the state or county could develop procedures for identifying the top five issues on voters' minds and enlist local college professors or pollsters to construct questions to be unbiased. Then, simply print the answers submitted by candidates. If they go over the word limit, only publish up to the word limit. That will keep them on task.

Now, candidates could refuse to answer. Or give the all too often heard "no-answer" answer. But let the voter decide its relevance. It would be telling if a school board member were asked, "Do you believe sexual orientation topics should be taught in school?" and they left it blank.

This one-stop shop for evaluating candidates could minimize the impact of PACs and Super PACs and candidate misleading advertisements and make it far easier for common folk like me to evaluate candidates and make informed votes. It would also minimize the impact of the media picking sides, giving positive attention to those who fit their bias and negative attention to those who don't. It could also pave the path for more citizen politicians because they would have a better chance of getting noticed and getting votes without media outlets pre-selecting based on incumbency, celebrity, or wealth.

Wouldn't it be refreshing to have some 55-year-old elected to office after a career in the real world? They are getting harder to come by.

Voting

Firstly, the notion that requiring voter ID is undemocratic is preposterous. It makes common sense for someone who wants to vote claiming to be themselves should demonstrate that they are, in fact, who they say they are. Anyone claiming that this stops citizens from voting is disrespecting the very citizens they claim to help. They are, in effect, telling them they are too stupid to have an ID. But don't worry; the saviors are here to help. Totally insulting.

If we are to minimize the incidence of voter fraud by misrepresenting who you are at the polls or by "mail-in," then require ID, like 46 of the 47 European countries do.

Secondly, for those who can't make it to the polls on election day due to work, travel, military service, or illness, let them vote absentee, as they do now. But let's do this online, shall we? Why can't we log on to the local election site, enter our ID number, be it a driver's license, passport, or other acceptable form of government-issued ID, and vote? You can open a bank account online because the bank uses tools to ensure you are who you say you are. Why can't county elections offices do the same?

This would all but eliminate the shenanigans with ballot stuffing or ballet harvesting, where partisans put ballot drop boxes in areas where there are groups of voters sympathetic to their cause while ignoring areas that are not. This is legal, but they are still shenanigans. Let the folks at the retirement home log on and vote. If they aren't able to log on at home, perhaps their local library or municipal office, where there could be people to assist them in logging on and voting.

Thirdly, to avoid the challenge of out-of-date voter registration, automatically de-register people who have not voted in a period of time, say three years. If you don't vote in three years but suddenly feel the urge, simply re-register. Hopefully online.

This should be easy to work out and minimize fraud that has been the mainstay of elections since Tammany Hall. Maybe there will be a very small amount of voters disenfranchised. But I was disenfranchised last election when I ordered an absentee ballot within the deadline because I was scheduled to be traveling on business, and my county elections office sent it to me after I had left. Where were my saviors on this travesty of voter disenfranchisement? If I was permitted to do so online, I could've voted from my hotel room in Jamestown, New York.

And imagine how easy it would be to count the vote. No more hanging chads. This makes so much sense that I'm at a loss as to why it needs to be said.

On Journalism

A free press has always been and still is an important lens of accountability for those who hold the greatest power in a society. In the U.S., the greatest power is held by our government(s), large companies and their executives, and the wealthy who can unduly influence people and elections through unchecked political action committees.

An example of the good that the free press can do is highlighting the Chinese government's treatment of the Uighurs, a Muslim minority concentrated in Xinjiang territory in Northwest China. The U.S. is acutely aware of how religious zealotry can significantly curtail freedoms, incite violence against non-believers, and mandate conformity. But it also can change governments—and China will have none of that.

So, they built "re-education camps," up to 85 of them by some reports, and interned over one million Uighurs. This has been widely reported in Western media. China's response was denial. Yet satellite photos released to the media clearly showed there were no camps pre-2017 and 85 in 2018.

Where was the Chinese state media on this? Here is a quote from the Chinese state-run *Global Times*:

> *"The turnaround in Xinjiang's security situation has avoided a great tragedy and saved countless lives, thanks to powerful Chinese law and the strong ruling power of the Communist Party of China. What the West has been hyping has destroyed numerous countries and regions. When the same evil influence was spreading in Xinjiang, it was decisively curbed."*[23]

The *Global Times* is the bullhorn for the Chinese Communist Party.

If the *Global Times* is your means of reading news, then you'd probably think, "Good job China!" Free press is vital to hold those in power to account.

The challenge is that a disproportionately large number of journalists favor one political viewpoint. For example, according to the Center for Public Integrity analysis of journalist donations to either the Clinton or Trump campaigns during the 2016 election, 96 percent of donations went to Clinton. That's a staggering number, considering that 49 percent of Americans identify as Democrats, and 40 percent identify as Republicans.

It is no surprise that we have created "camps" in the media we consume. According to AllSides, most of what we consider "mainstream media," i.e., ABC, NBC, CBS, National Public Radio (NPR), *NY Times, Washington Post*, and CNN are far left or left-leaning[24]. NPR is partially funded by taxpayer dollars and could not manage a centrist rating.

There are not that many "mainstream" networks in the leaning right or far right category. In fact, many in the Centrist column are considered right-leaning sheerly based on how heavily left the media see-saw tilts. If media outlets are considered right or far right, they are marginalized because media is so dominated by the left.

Worse, because of the lack of balance, if you lean right, you're more likely to watch Fox News than CNN, so you hear one side of the story and have less information at your disposal to make informed decisions.

As media consumers, this is our fault. We are voting media coverage with our eyeballs, and those eyeballs are not consuming much of The Christian Science Monitor or NewsNation, which are consistently ranked as balanced by AllSides.

How Do Journalists Slant News?

In 2018, Georgia had a humdinger of a gubernatorial election between Democrat Stacey Abrams, a statehouse representative, and Republican Brian Kemp, the then Secretary of State whose responsibility, among other responsibilities, was monitoring elections. Kemp won, but not without a post-election fight by Abrams. The following post-election statement by Abrams was carried in a November 2018 CNN article:

> *"Make no mistake, the former secretary of state was deliberate and intentional in his actions," Abrams said. "I know that eight years of systemic disenfranchisement, disinvestment, and incompetence had its desired effect on the electoral process in Georgia."*[25]

In 2020, then-President Donald Trump lobbed claims of a rigged election. Here is what CNN wrote about those claims in November 2020:

> *"A senior federal election security official who was appointed by President Donald Trump has blasted the President's false post-election claims, calling them 'baffling', 'laughable' and 'insulting'.*[26]

Firstly, CNN significantly covered Trump's false claims and did not seem to pay much, if any, attention to Abrams'. At least not enough to label them false in the stories they ran in the election's aftermath. Secondly, note that CNN carried Abrams' false post-election claims without looking into them or labeling them false or unproven. However, CNN *was* quick to point out that Trump's statements were false.

Truth be told, both were false, unproven, and have been subsequently debunked. But you wouldn't know it from the CNN coverage. False claims were seemingly the sole domain of Trump—if the sum total of news coverage were taken at face value and you paid attention to the labels within the articles.

This type of bias that adds either editorial or fact-checked words ("false claims") conveniently supporting the editorial bias of the news organization is ubiquitous in journalism, and it is rarely called out. Let's call it ***Micro-Editorializing***. The news was covered. It was accurate. However, the difference in how one false claim was handled versus the other false claim lay bare where the news organization falls on the right-left spectrum.

Another form of micro-editorializing for video and radio news is the vocal tone and inflection of the person delivering the news. For example, Robin Meade, the long-time anchor for CNN's now-defunct HLN Network, reported on a young boy who ran up to Pope Francis during a mass. While difficult in writing to describe her tonality, she said, "Pope Francis was in the middle of a service when a little boy ran up AND JOINED HIM."[27] She said it in such a way that she thought it was cute and acceptable. I'm not suggesting she was wrong. It was cute. But she inserted her opinion without so much as a change in the words of the report. Imagine the inflection micro-editorializing can have on more important topics based on the bias of either the news outlet or the reporter.

Should it be that way?

Another form of bias in journalism is what is covered versus what is ignored. The January 6th commission wrapped up in December 2022. A fringe right-wing group that played a key role in the rioting was the Proud Boys. A search of the Fox News website, using "Proud Boys" and limiting the search to December 2022, resulted in articles with the following headlines:

"Leftist mob riots after Charlie Kirk shows up at campus, tries to shut down free speech event"

"Biden's domestic social media surveillance alarms major civil rights group: 'Do not need a new war on terror'."

"Pennsylvania school board member to resign over statement rejecting 'cis White male' for president"

Meanwhile, a CNN search on "Proud Boys" for December 2022 resulted in the following headlines:

"First transcripts from Jan. 6 committee reveal key witnesses refusing to testify"

"Why did some Proud Boys dress up like Antifa on January 6?"

"Trial begins for Proud Boys leaders charged with seditious conspiracy"

Why does Fox News, listed by AllSides as "Right," barely cover what should have been a well-covered story on the Proud Boys after the January 6 commission issued its report? CNN, listed by AllSides as "Left," is all over it. Why? Because Proud Boys is a far-right group that serves as a needle in the eye to people on the political right. A desirable outcome for a "Left" news outlet and an inconvenient truth for the "Right."

I will label this type of journalistic bias as ***Ignore or Explore***, depending on how convenient or inconvenient the news is to the news outlet's bias. If I were looking for the latest news on the Proud Boys and the role they played in the January 6 riots, I would have to dig deep on Fox while CNN slapped me in the face with it.

We deserve better.

Another form of journalistic bias I will describe is by way of example. There is a conservative-leaning satire site called *The Babylon Bee*. You may have heard about it because it was one of those Twitter accounts that was banned by the social media platform prior to the Elon Musk takeover.

One of their satirical videos was about a college student going door-to-door to collect money to pay off her student loans. This was poking fun at the Biden Administration's attempt to absolve students and recent graduates of some of their student debt.

In the sketch, the student was a young recent grad who was a gender studies major, engaging with a factory foreman at his home asking for money because the knowledge she had, which she claimed was deeper knowledge than the foreman, betters society and, therefore, he should be obliged to pay off her loan.

The student checked all the stereotypical boxes for wokeism, including voice, dress, entitlement, and air of superiority. She was a cartoonish character. The foreman, on the other hand, was your everyman, common sense, dressed the part, with a modest house, holding a beer, and a modest car in the driveway. In other words, the student was outlandish, and the foreman was someone we could relate to.

This is how bias creeps into journalism. When representing a viewpoint consistent with the news outlet's bias, they engage with someone we respect and can relate to. Representing the opposing viewpoint is some buffoon that, either through looks, words, voice, past works, or temperament, is easily dismissed by the viewer because they are somehow different and difficult to relate to. That is why you rarely see Thomas Sowell on CNN or Paul Krugman on Fox representing opposing views. They are too respectable.

I call this bias ***Opposing View Buffoonery***. When you see someone with crazy hair representing the opposing view, you know the media outlet's bias. It shouldn't be so.

How Should It Be?

Journalists purport to have standards, and the standard setter for U.S. journalists is the Society for Professional Journalists or SPJ.

On their website, the SPJ's code of ethics reads:

> *"Members of the Society of Professional Journalists believe that public enlightenment is the forerunner of justice and the foundation of democracy. Ethical journalism strives to ensure the free exchange of information that is accurate, fair and thorough. An ethical journalist acts with integrity.*
>
> *"The Society declares these four principles as the foundation of ethical journalism and encourages their use in its practice by all people in all media."*

The four principles mentioned are: Seek Truth and Report It; Minimize Harm; Act Independently; Be Accountable and Transparent.[28]

Each of these four principles had further details that started with "Journalists should." If a journalist asks you how you think they should dispense of their duties, tell them you would like them to do so according to the SPJ Code of Ethics.

Most would probably respond that they follow the SPJ Code of Ethics—at least the letter of the code, if not the spirit of it. A case in point would be how the Three Mile Island (TMI) nuclear accident is covered. TMI recently shut down because its then owner, Exelon Energy, could not operate it profitably. TMI, as most know, had a partial meltdown in its Reactor #2 in 1979 but was operating Reactor #1 since the accident, at least prior to its closing.

In an NPR article regarding the fight to keep it open titled "40 Years After A Partial Nuclear Meltdown, A New Push To Keep Three Mile Island Open"[29], the reporter described the accident. It wasn't until paragraph eight that the article stated, "…in the end, it wasn't a disaster." Only a small amount of radiation was released. The radiation released caused no long-term health problems. Many readers may be surprised because of how this "nuclear meltdown" is covered.

According to a 2022 study[30] from the Reuters Institute for the Study of Journalism, only 51% of consumers who shared an online news story actually read the whole article, while 26% read part, and 22% looked at just the headline or a few lines. And these are the people so moved by it they shared it. What are the chances that the average reader of the NPR story got to the eighth paragraph? The context of the TMI accident not being a disaster was buried in the story. In my experience, this is a common occurrence with TMI coverage. Why?

Journalists should report in fact and context. Why do journalists pick sides? They should be on the side of truth, both in letter and in spirit. Highlighting some facts that support your bias and hiding facts that are inconvenient to that bias is hardly in keeping with the principle of "seek truth and report it."

This is not to say that issues having two sides get fifty-fifty treatment—or even treatment in proportion to its occurrence.

The 2020 murder of George Floyd got significantly more attention than police homicides of unarmed black men occurring statistically. But this instance, in its brazenness by the perpetrator and the indifference from the other officers, merited significantly more attention because police should be held to higher standards in how they carry out their responsibilities. Their responsibilities impact all of us. Much more so than, say, a warehouse worker or a law clerk. So, the level of media attention was warranted, although it gave the general public the false impression that this was a common occurrence.

But what if the media *wanted* its viewers to believe it was a common occurrence? The commonsense question is, why? Why would a media outlet want you to believe what was uncommon is common?

This is part and parcel of the Ignore or Explore journalistic bias. Report on something that fits your bias in such frequency that viewers believe it is common, even prevalent when objective analysis of the data clearly shows it is not. And the data is not hard to find. But often, journalists would have to peel back the onion a little further than a social media post by a partisan.

Is it journalistic laziness? Or does the journalist or media outlet have an agenda? Why would you position something as true that is untrue? This is a commonsense question.

As media consumers, we should demand answers and relegate partisan rags to the checkout aisle where they belong.

That is what I would demand from journalists, and I hope you will join me. Change will only occur if we change our media consumption. Do we want to know what is true? Or validate what we believe to be true, correct or not?

On Healthcare

In April 2019, Mick Jagger, the frontman for the Rolling Stones, was on a World Tour with the band and preparing for the tour's North American leg. Except his doctors advised against it. Why? He was diagnosed with a heart condition, likely aortic stenosis or a narrow heart valve. It would make sense to diagnose this while on tour. Aside from Jagger's age at that time, he was likely exerting himself onstage—moving like Jagger, so to speak.

The remedy for aortic stenosis is a minimally invasive procedure called transcatheter aortic valve replacement, or TAVR. Jagger is a British citizen, and the United Kingdom has a universal healthcare system called the National Health Service or NHS. NHS is funded with tax dollars that equate to approximately 4.5% of an average Britons pay.[31] Lest someone tell you it is free, it is not, nor is any other universal healthcare system on the planet.

So Jagger should rest easy, right? There would be no or minimal marginal cost to have his TAVR procedure. Except he chose to have the procedure done in the United States. Why?

According to the British Heart Foundation, in 2021, nearly one in four heart procedure candidates waited over four months.[32] Mick was on tour and couldn't wait. So, he went to an American specialist. According to a 2020 National Institute of Health (NIH) study, sixty-two percent of Canadians experienced a greater than 30-day wait time from primary care physician referral to when they saw the specialist; for Britons, it was fifty-five percent, and for Americans, it was thirty-one percent.[33]

Wait times are a very common problem in countries with nationalized health insurance. If the marginal cost to a patient is zero or near zero, then the system will be overused. And since it is government-run, then expenses are controlled by decree—as in, "We are the only game in town, and we will only reimburse you, Mr. or Ms. Doctor, this much for this procedure." This leads to labor shortages as the long road to becoming a doctor or nurse is not as financially rewarding when the government fixes your prices.

It causes a supply (labor, equipment, facilities) shortage as governments manage budgets across a significantly large part of the economy. And it creates demand issues as the marginal cost to a patient to get that MRI to make super sure the doctor's diagnosis is correct, is nothing, or is near nothing.

Since time immemorial, the one thing that has proven effective in bringing supply and demand into equilibrium is price. And the best way to control price is through competition. And in a nationalized health system, there is little.

CEOWorld Magazine performs an annual review[34] of national healthcare systems and assigns a score based on the overall quality of the healthcare system, including healthcare infrastructure; healthcare professionals (doctors, nursing staff, and other health workers) competencies; cost; quality medicine availability, and government readiness. In 2022, the top-rated healthcare systems were South Korea, Taiwan, and Denmark. The U.S. was 30th, behind Mexico and ahead of Lithuania.

What the top three had in common were single-payer systems. This wasn't nationalized healthcare, meaning the government runs the facilities, and the providers are government employees. But there is centralized insurance. This has proved effective. In Taiwan, for example, administrative costs are less than 2 percent. According to a 2020 research report based on 2017 data, the U.S. administrative costs are 34.2 percent, or nearly $2,500 per insured.[35]

Clearly, something must change. But what? One thing we learned during the pandemic is Americans are dogmatically independent. We don't like being told what to do. Imagine being married to a single-payer health insurance system, run by the U.S. government, that convenes a panel to determine if you need a knee replacement. Or the U.S. government telling medical providers what they will and won't pay for, and how much they will pay them. And once we do it, it would be nearly impossible to undo.

The United Kingdom, by way of example of the predictable consequence of a nationalized health system, is trying to systematically raise the age when you can buy cigarettes. If you have vices that are bad for your health, and you incur little financial cost for your health decisions because that cost is cast onto society, then society will work to reduce your freedom to engage in your unhealthy behavior.

Governments work very hard to consolidate power and don't have a strong history of, once consolidated, giving it back. No, the U.S. way must be different. Healthcare is a significant and growing part of our economy. Give up the keys to Washington D.C.? No, thank you.

So what should wc do?

First, focus on what is wrong. Focus on the steep administrative costs in our system. Costs that are screaming to be wrung out. How often do you speak to people in a medical office who have very little to do with your health? Almost always, I would guess. These are the people in billing—filling out forms, interfacing with insurance companies, and tracking down insureds for payments not covered by insurance. One person comes in for a regular checkup and walks out with a $200 bill, another with a $300 bill for the same service. Why the difference?

It's what the insurer negotiates with the provider network.

What our system sorely lacks is transparency. When you buy a car, you research quality, dependability, look, and price. When you buy a medical service, you're told what to do by a provider, you do it, and then find out the price. You have no idea when you decide what it will cost out-of-pocket. This must end.

If you go to the doctor with a sore knee after a pickup soccer game, you may be diagnosed with a hyperextended knee. The doc says he or she is 90% sure that is what ails you and anti-inflammatory and rest are the best treatments. But if you want to be 100% sure, you'll need an MRI.

If an MRI was free to you on the margin, meaning your health insurance (private or government) pays all of it, you are likely to take it. Why not be 100% sure? It costs nothing but the time demanded of you. Multiply that decision hundreds of thousands of times across the country, and you can see that "free" healthcare overtaxes the system.

If you knew that the MRI was $1,000, and your insurance plan would only cover half, now you have a different decision. Is it worth the marginal $500 for the doctor to be 100% certain? Even if the cash was stashed in a Health Savings Account ("HSA"), you still see it draining from the account. An account that you own.

With technology today, even with different providers and different health plans, there is little reason why an app on our phone, likely designed and provided by our insurance carrier, can't tell us what a medical procedure will cost prior to the decision to undertake it. What other areas of your life do you not compare cost to benefit? Medical decisions should be no different.

This requires some level of uniformity in procedure codes and provider types so such relational databases can be built and easily accessible by those participating in the medical system. Here is where the government can play a constructive role. Developing standards for uniform data. The Dodd-Frank Act of 2010 required the U.S. government to propose standards for sharing financial information among financial intermediaries. In 2023, the Consumer Financial Protection Bureau did so. Why can't our government do this for medical records, procedures, and costs?

You want to drive medical costs down? Make medical costs transparent so patients make medical AND cost/benefit decisions.

Insurance is a shared cost system. The sick are subsidized by the healthy. In the United States, insurance is optional. So, if you are a healthy person or low-income and can't afford health insurance, you might not have it. This takes healthy people out of the overall insurance pool.

The Federal Emergency Medical Treatment and Labor Act of 1986 requires hospitals to care for patients with an emergency or potentially emergency medical condition, regardless of ability to pay. This provides further incentive to otherwise healthy people to not insure. If something serious happens, they can go to the emergency room and get treatment.

According to Excel Health, the cost of uncompensated healthcare in the U.S. was $44.4 billion between 2015-17.[36] Hospitals compensate for this cost through government programs, charity programs, and increased prices for insured patients. Whether the actual patient who, by choice or circumstance, has no medical insurance pushes the cost to a taxpayer, a charitable giver, or his or her fellow patient does not change the perverse incentive to push costs from the patient to someone else.

So, as much as I am pro-choice, pro-freedom, and decentralization of decisions, we must compel our citizens to have health insurance. This is much like we compel drivers to have car insurance. We need healthy people in the pool to subsidize sick people. It's the nature of insurance.

But I am not proposing a single-payer system where the government is the pivot for your medical coverage or for how much a doctor can charge you. Let's build on the current decentralized system with common sense improvements, like the cost transparency previously mentioned. And the standards-based medical procedures codes, medical provider codes, and records retention and availability.

In fact, private companies can store medical records owned by patients and accessed by providers and insurers only with the permission of the patient. This would make medical records more standard and portable. If you want to fire your doctor, disable their access to your medical records and grant access to your new doctor.

Standardization could also streamline medical billing and reduce the myriad of medical administrators that drive up the unacceptable levels of administrative costs in the U.S. system. If I took my child for a polio vaccine, the procedure code and charges would be sent from doctor to insurer, and payment would occur without human intervention. Rejections would be known immediately and for what reason. Patients would know going in what their financial responsibility for that visit would be prior to entering the doctor's office. The difference between insurance payment and the procedure could be paid for on the spot with the insured's HSA debit card.

Insurance companies could be audited to ensure they pay for what they promise in coverage. A common insurance company trick is to not reimburse or to hold reimbursement due to some administrative error so they don't have to pay or delay payment. Those "deny" decisions would happen immediately and could be rectified quickly by the provider.

Insurance companies that don't deliver what they promise can be fined by the government or privately sued. Their payment record would be on display prior to any patient selecting them as their insurance carrier or before any provider signs on to be a preferred provider in their network. Insurance companies would have ample motivation to deliver what they promise.

True competition will come when the payer of services is the consumer of services. Look at auto insurance. We're forced to buy it, and we do so privately. Bad drivers pay more than good drivers. And the Camaro owner pays more than the Camry owner.

In my business (consulting), I told our office manager that we should get out of the benefits business. Can't we pay employees a certain pre-tax dollar benefit and allow them to shop in competitive marketplaces for their own employee benefits? So, if they want a Cadillac health plan, they can buy it and make up the difference. If they want a minimum health plan that includes dental and vision, they can do that, too. They can basically take their employee benefit dollars and shop as they wish without the stigma of doing it as an "individual" versus a "group."

I propose a required minimum basic coverage that encourages preventative care and keeps families out of bankruptcy should they fall ill. This might be a high-deductible HSA plan that has a maximum out-of-pocket (MOOP) per annum per family of about $10,000, adjusted for inflation. There must be language to limit political influence in this law. The Basic Plan should be simple and protect families from bankruptcy due to extraordinary medical expenses while encouraging preventative care.

I like HSA plans because it puts individual skin in the game. You want to load the shopping cart with Oreos or smoke a pack a day? It will cost you much more than those that don't; skin in the game. Put behavior and cost of the behavior as close to the individual as possible so there is a consequence. Accountability is crucial to the success of healthcare. Offloading responsibilities for people's choices to "society" doesn't make common sense.

States can have overlays to keep state control—especially since the Federal mandate will be basic. But regulation and enforcement of the national law would be national. Regulation of overlays can be state-based. So, if California wants to jack up the prices of plans to include medical, recreational, and Cheech and Chong level marijuana use, it's on Californians. We shouldn't charge Georgians for it.

Medicaid should be transitory. We are creating a lifelong needy class in our society. The more dependence on government, the more we need favor from the government bureaucrat, which is dangerous. Check history. However, if states want to keep subsidizing people who aren't employed, lack the basic plan, and have lots of protest time, it's their choice.

Competition for employees would be much more transparent, as most employers would opt to provide a benefits dollar amount so employees can shop in the various marketplaces with those dollars. And those benefits would be portable and not tied to employment. Employees would no longer have to remain anchored to jobs they dislike just to "keep the benefits."

The objective is to create a competitive, transparent, effective, and efficient healthcare system so we don't cede power and control to one or a few entities we are beholden to. Why would we give a bureaucrat the keys to our health?

On Taxes

A couple opens a milkshake stand in Anytown, USA. They form three lines for customers. Line 1 prices milkshakes at $5 per shake, representing the couple's cost plus a profit. Line 2 gives the shakes away. Line 3 charges $15. One hundred people show up for shakes on opening day. Which line do they get in?

Living in our country is voluntary. If we don't like it, we can leave. If we don't think we are being treated fairly, that the deck is stacked against us, we can leave. There's a cost to that decision. We have family and friends here. We speak the language. We are familiar with our surroundings and enjoy the conveniences we've come to expect living here. And the United States is a country where you can rise above your station if you choose to put in the work—at least it is as of this writing.

So when the government forces people to get into the $15 milkshake line, most comply. That shake line is required to pay for the free line. Because those shakes, as we all know, are not free. And the longer the free line gets, the more that couple must rely on Line 3 to cover costs and profit. If Line 3 doesn't get longer, then the couple must charge more. As the price escalates, there will be fewer people in Line 3. Now, the couple will have to start looking to Line 1 to make the shortfall, convincing those in that line that it is only their "fair share."

This is what the former British prime minister Margaret Thatcher meant when she said, "Sooner or later you will run out of other people's money."

However, if Line 2, the free shake line, is considerably longer than Line 3, the fifteen-dollar line, and all customers of the milkshake stand voted democratically about who should pay what, what would happen?

Most likely, the considerably longer line would support continuing to get their shakes for free. And they would likely further support charging Line 3 even more to cover the eventual shortfall to the couple that owned the milkshake stand. Line 2 might even paint those in Line 3 as greedy, cheaters, and privileged.

If that doesn't work, Line 2 would want the couple to absorb the shortfall. Calling them "Big Shake" capitalists greedy for profit. If successful, this would likely lead to the owners closing the stand. No more milkshakes in Anytown USA.

Making the situation even worse is that people in Line 1, the $5 shake line, who are at the precipice of being forced into Line 3, will take action to stay in Line 1, stunting their economic mobility. Likewise, those just over the threshold in Line 3 will try to get back into Line 1. Those in Line 2 will try to stay put. A highly progressive tax system sucks the incentives out of upward economic mobility—a situation that suits those who benefit from long lines in Line 2 just fine.

Now you understand where we are in terms of the U.S. tax system. We have a majority who contribute relatively little to all levels of government, voting to keep paying little while charging others more. The so-called, "don't tax me, don't tax thee, tax that fellow under the tree."

According to the Tax Foundation, the U.S. tax and transfer system is highly progressive, meaning the higher you go up the income and wealth ladder, the more you are taxed beyond the benefits you receive from all levels of government.[37]

The bottom quintile of households faces an effective federal, state, and local rate of 10.1 percent, while the middle quintile bears 22.4 percent, and the top quintile faces a 41.4 percent burden. Even though much of this progressivity stems from the federal government, a similar effect is visible at the state and local level as well, with state and local effective rates ranging from 7.8 percent for the bottom quintile to 12.1 percent for the top quintile, according to the Tax Foundation.

In fact, on average, households in the top quintile had a total estimated tax burden of $125,748 in 2019, consisting of $89,055 in federal taxes and $36,693 in state and local taxes, according to the Tax Foundation study. The middle and bottom quintiles bore a much smaller total tax burden of $24,451 and $5,524, respectively. These tax burdens include taxes paid on economic activity underwritten by transfer payments, such as individuals paying corporate taxes baked into the prices of goods and services purchased from those corporations.

Corporations don't pay taxes. They collect them from their customers. Those who support higher corporate taxes effectively support a more regressive tax system. General Mills annualized income taxes of $693 million are not paid by General Mills. It's paid for by the people who eat Chex Mix.

What do you consider your "fair share?"

We are taxed enough.

If you think each household should pay equally, then to support the Federal government's $6.134 trillion in outlays in fiscal 2023, the 131 million U.S. households would each owe $46,671. If you pay less than that in federal income tax, fees, and your share of corporate taxes (which equates to approximately 10% of federal tax receipts), you wouldn't be paying your "fair share," according to a simplistically objective definition of fair.

If you're okay with the current tax system but want to pay more—and why shouldn't we because we don't demand federal representatives balance the books—we would have to contribute $13,670 more per household. In the fiscal year 2023, the federal government rang up a deficit of $1.695 trillion.[38] Instead of reducing government expenditures, our representatives will be looking for that fellow under the tree.

Spoiler alert—there are not nearly enough fellows under the tree. But it makes for a good sound bite. And we fall for it. The U.S. Representative incumbency rate for 2022, according to Open Secrets, was 94.5%.[39] We seem comfortable spending beyond our means because we think someone else will pay for it. Our current federal debt, 35 trillion dollars, equates to over 266 thousand dollars per U.S. household.

From 2015 through 2023, federal revenues grew 0.7% per year, from $4.2 trillion to $4.44 trillion. This included the tax cuts enacted in 2017 and a pandemic. Tax revenues for fiscal 2017, prior to the 2017 tax cuts going into effect, were $3.76 trillion. After they went into effect, tax revenues were $3.97 trillion. Taxes were cut, and revenues went up. This is what's known as the Laffer Curve, where increased economic activity outweighs the arithmetic effect of lowering tax rates, resulting in greater revenues to the government. The challenge is it is difficult to know where we are on the curve.

Although revenues grew 0.7% per year from 2015-2023, expenditures rose 3.7% per year during the same period, from $4.6 trillion to the aforementioned $6.1 trillion. As a percentage of Gross Domestic Product (GDP), revenues ranged between 17%-19% while expenditures ranged between 20%-23%. Revenues have been in this range since the 1950s. It's expenditures that would seemingly need to come down.

Reducing expenditures, however, would have a disparate impact on our hypothetical milkshake Line 2, since they are the greater beneficiaries of government spending. The Tax Foundation estimates that households in the bottom earnings quintile received an effective net tax-and-transfer benefit of $1.27 for every dollar they earned in income—in other words, a tax-and-transfer rate of -127.0 percent. Households in the top quintile, on the other hand, experienced an effective reduction of $0.31 for every dollar they earned in income.

Do we raise taxes to maintain spending? According to Mercatus Center research, under the American Recovery and Reinvestment Act of 2009, the federal government spent roughly $300 billion (2.1 percent of GDP) extra in both 2009 and 2010. The extra $600 billion of public spending cost $900 billion in private spending when considering the spending multiplier of 0.6 over two years. A 2011 study found that increased government spending reduced private-sector portions of GDP, assuming the extra government spending must be paid for by taxpayers.[40] A spending multiplier of one is neutral; over one is beneficial, while under one is detrimental.

In other words, it is better for a dollar to be spent in the private sector than by the government. This makes sense because a dollar sent to government must be inefficiently allocated based on politics versus the greatest return to the individual spending it. And that government-spent dollar must pass through a bureaucracy, with each level skimming as it passes. The U.S. Department of Education has 4,400 employees and a $68 billion annual budget, as an example.

Government spending is necessary for national defense, reasonable regulation, law and order, and social welfare—things necessary for a free and orderly society that would not receive adequate private investment. But as an economic accelerator, it falls short to private investment.

We should not be anxious to contribute more to government because of this inefficiency. No, we send enough.

If raising revenue must be part of the solution to the debt hole our politicians have dug, and we are complicit in their digging, it makes sense for revenue increases to be two-pronged: 1) economic growth and 2) tax compliance.

According to the White House, tax receipts are projected to grow at an average annual rate of 5.3 percent between 2023 and 2027, rising to $5,695.9 billion. Receipts are projected to rise to $7,083.0 billion in 2032, growing at an average annual rate of 4.5 percent between 2027 and 2032. This growth is largely due to assumed increases in incomes resulting from both real economic growth and inflation and the expiration of the tax cuts passed in 2017.[41] And as pointed out, if the economic impact of raising taxes outweighs the mathematical impact of taking money from the private sector and sending it to the government, these revenue growth estimates may be optimistic.

Tax compliance, where people and businesses pay what they actually owe under current tax law, would seem to yield little at the margin. Not so. For tax years 2021 and 2020, the latest to receive such IRS estimates, the projected gross "tax gap" soared to $688 billion and $601 billion, respectively. That marks a significant jump compared to years past — with gross tax gap projections standing at $550 billion for 2017-2019 and $496 billion for 2014-2016.[42]

This is why the current president's administration proposed an increase in the IRS budget to amp up tax compliance. This makes sense. There are a number of reasons why taxes go uncollected, including:

- Non-filing: Some people fail to file their tax returns at all.
- Underreporting: Some people underreport their income or overstate their deductions.
- Underpayment: Some people pay less tax than they owe, either intentionally or unintentionally.
- Complex tax laws: The tax code is complex, and it can be difficult for taxpayers to understand and comply with all the rules.

- Limited IRS resources: The IRS is understaffed and underfunded, which makes it difficult to audit taxpayers and collect unpaid taxes.

This tax gap has a number of negative consequences. It reduces the government's revenue, which means that there is less money available for important programs and services and deficit reduction. It also creates an unfair advantage for those who do not pay their taxes, and it can undermine public confidence in the tax system. If you pay your taxes according to tax law, and your neighbor does not and gets away with it, your motivation to continue paying what you legally owe will decline, and the tax gap will grow.

This is common sense.

When the presidential administration proposed increasing the IRS budget for tax compliance, it was met with staunch opposition by the opposing party. The complexity of our tax code likely results in households and businesses that would otherwise comply but make mistakes along the way. If they happen to be political opponents, the IRS could target them to discourage opposition.

The first root cause of the relatively large tax gap is to simplify the tax code and compliance with the tax code so compliance becomes much easier.

There will still be those who choose not to comply. In 2022, the IRS' budget was $14.3 billion and employed 79,000 people. That is one agent per 1,600 households and $115 per household for tax compliance. It could be enough if there were significant increases in technology to focus on the greatest tax cheats. Technology could also be used to ensure that IRS agents were not put on the case by political motivations like they did when they harassed conservative not-for-profits in 2013.[43]

Does it make sense to raise taxes on those who comply to compensate for those who don't?

Reducing the tax gap by half would go a long way to a balanced federal budget and reducing overall government debt, leading to more private investment to fuel growth in the United States economy to maintain our position as an economic superpower, which translates to a military superpower.

It's not just the United States that depends on this status. The U.S. military is the greatest force for peace the world has ever seen. Despots loathe it because it limits their ability to put people under their power. The world depends on it.

Consistent deficit spending weakens us, as will taking money out of the private economy to fund government spending that is inefficient or ineffective and weakens our position as an economic superpower.

We pay enough in taxes. We should solve for living within our means.

On Abortion

In August 2022, Kansas, a state that was 44% Republican and 26% Democrat, voted 59% to 41% to retain the state's constitutional guarantee to a woman's right to an abortion. The chief medical officer of a local Planned Parenthood office said, "I'm so proud to be a provider in this community. I'm so proud that I get to serve this community. I moved here two years ago from Chicago with the intention of providing abortion care in a place where there were not a lot of providers."[44]

Before you close the book because I struck an ideological nerve of those either for or against abortion, know that I supported the overturning of Roe v. Wade because I am biased toward pushing power to the lowest levels of government as practicably as possible. In this case, let the states decide.

Additionally, I believe in freedom. If I were to support abortion limits in my state, it would be a reasonable time period for the mother to decide to abort or not to abort, such as 14 weeks. I think abortion kills a baby. But this is an argument to be made within our families, churches, and our own collective consciences—not by a politician's or judge's decree.

We cannot ignore, however, this most important question: What about the babies?

In 2016, Doritos ran a Super Bowl ad of a couple at the hospital, the wife about to give birth to a baby. The disinterested husband stood idly by, noshing on Doritos. The baby, shown through the ultrasound, was attentively following the dad waving a chip. The wife grabs the chip and throws it. In response, the baby flies out of the womb. Funny, right? Not so to NARAL, formerly known as the National Abortion Rights Action League, who denounced it for "humanizing fetuses."

According to the Guttmacher Institute, a pro-abortion organization that likely is the best source for accurate abortion information in the United States because the Centers for Disease Control (CDC) doesn't collect abortion data from every state, there were over 930,000 abortions in the United States in 2020. Some would have us believe that terminating these babies was the result of rape, incest, or the health of the mother. At least based on how many news outlets cover the subject and nearly every pro-abortion advocate argues it.

According to the Lozier Institute's analysis of eight states that collect information on why a woman is seeking an abortion, less than five percent reported seeking to end their pregnancy as a result of rape, incest, or their own health.[45] Why do news outlets report like it is far more common?

The good news is that 930,000 is much lower than abortion's peak of 1.6 million babies aborted in 1990. As a result of education and birth control, we are aborting nearly 700,000 fewer babies. All while Roe v. Wade was the de facto law of the land.

Not a law, actually. But a 1973 Supreme Court ruling overturning a Texas ban on abortion. Roe v. Wade cited the right to privacy in the 14th Amendment to the Constitution as the basis for its ruling. Ironic because it was Republicans who championed the 14th Amendment, and it is Republicans who generally disdain Roe v. Wade.

Another positive to discuss regarding abortion, if we can claim positives, is that it lowers crime. You read that right. According to Steven Levitt and Stephen Dubner in their 2005 book *Freakonomics*, 30 percent to

40 percent of the decrease in crime in the 1990s was the result of the legalization of abortion.[46]

This makes sense. Unwanted babies are at higher risk to grow up to be criminals. So, if we abort the unwanted babies, ipso facto, fewer criminals. Levitt, after performing the study a second time because he was criticized for a technical error in the first study, came to the same conclusion the second time. In a recent *Freakonomics* podcast, he said, surprisingly, that the hate generated from each study came more from the pro-abortion camp. Killing babies before they turn into criminals must not fit their worldview. Sort of like *Minority Report* in real life. *Minority Report* was a Tom Cruise movie where they punished would-be criminals before they committed the crime.

Main arguments for abortion are: body integrity (my body, my choice), socio-economic impact, and women's health.

My body, my choice is the rallying cry for pro-abortion folks. Aside from the inconsistency among many of these same people arguing to compel others to get Covid-19 vaccines during the pandemic, this is likely the crux of the Roe decision. Shouldn't a woman have the right to choose to carry the baby or not? It's her body. And the court saw it as a privacy issue.

Fair enough. This does, however, ignore the rights of the father, who presumably has a stake in the aborting of his child because the mother does not want to carry it. But let's assume they are on the same page. The pregnancy is unwanted, so let's end it.

I recently read an article about the legal proceedings regarding Scott Peterson, the Californian who was convicted of killing his wife, Lacey. In the article, it said he was also convicted of the murder of his unborn child. Now, if he was convicted of murdering an unborn child, logic would dictate that California thinks an unborn child is a person worth being born. California!

According to the National Right to Life Committee, 30 states carry full unborn victims laws, and another eight carry partial unborn victims laws. California's partial unborn victims law that convicted Peterson reads, "Murder is the unlawful killing of a human being, or a fetus, with malice aforethought." The words "or a fetus" were added by the legislature in 1970. The California Supreme Court later interpreted "fetus" to apply "beyond the embryonic stage of seven to eight weeks."[47]

My home state of Pennsylvania has a full unborn victims law that reads: "An individual commits criminal homicide in the first, second, or third-degree, or voluntary manslaughter of an 'unborn child' if the individual intentionally, knowingly, recklessly, or negligently causes the death of an unborn child." This law was challenged in 2006 by various constituencies using, among other arguments, Roe v Wade. The Pennsylvania Supreme Court rejected all these arguments and upheld the law.

This is in-your-face hypocrisy. The killing of the unborn child is bad... unless the carrying mother decides it's not. My body, my choice.

But what about the baby? Couldn't we change our minds as to the timing of the choice to be immediately prior to conception rather than when the baby is forming in the mother?

The second argument for abortion is the socio-economic argument, partially analyzed by Dubner and Levitt regarding the impact on crime rates. There's also the socio-economic impact on the mother. A key reason to abort the child is the mother or couple is not prepared to bring a child into the world and raise it. It would have a materially negative impact on the financial well-being of the parent(s). By forcing the mother to have the baby, we are relegating her, and possibly the father, to economic immobility. We're anchoring them to poverty.

This is true. There are many actions people can and do take to torpedo their economic mobility. Illicit drug use and/or alcohol abuse, criminal behavior, and so forth. Becoming pregnant and carrying an unwanted child is the only one I can think of that requires a life to be terminated to avoid the consequences of the behavior. But in terms of impact on the parent(s) economic status, the argument makes sense.

This consequence can be mitigated through adoption. There are an estimated two million couples in the United States wanting to adopt. Perhaps politicians on both sides of this issue can analyze the laws on their state's books and the regulations imposed to enforce those laws to make adoption an easier and less expensive option for the biological and adoptive parent(s). If we could save more babies, isn't it worth it?

The last argument relates to women's health. According to a 2021 statement by the United Nations Office of the High Commissioner on Human Rights, "25 million unsafe abortions take place annually, resulting in approximately 47,000 deaths every year, primarily in developing countries and among members of socioeconomically disadvantaged and marginalized populations."[48] This represents 0.19% of the 25 million unsafe abortions if my math is correct.

The missive from the High Commissioner was extremely biased and never mentioned the babies. It did not say that abortions were necessary for the health of the mother other than to say it threatens her health because she would seek an "unsafe" abortion if a "safe" one was not available.

Nor did it mention that if the mother did not have the abortion at all, it would jeopardize her health. In fact, it's total argument that "safe" abortion should be accessible, and the reason it is inaccessible is European colonialism and the promotion of a patriarchal power structure. I'm not kidding. Read their words from 2021:

> *"The systematic denial of timely access to safe abortion services is discriminatory and reflects a gendered power struggle involving the instrumentalization of women's bodies aimed at subjecting them to a patriarchal agenda. Patriarchal oppression is not specific to any country or region: it is universal. Colonialism has perpetuated the patriarchal control and oppression of societies, especially the control of women's sexuality."*
>
> - United Nations Human Rights Office of the High Commissioner

I first thought the letter was written by a Cal Berkeley undergrad.

What the letter does not state is that if the woman does not have the abortion, her health is at risk. The case, as they made it, is that her freedom is at risk. Her health would be at risk only because she would seek an illegal and likely more dangerous abortion.

This certainly makes sense. But the health argument in the U.S. makes us believe that if the mother of the unborn child was not permitted to abort it, she might have some health calamity. I know of no argument made by either pro- or anti-abortion camps that claim medical procedures following miscarriages or ectopic pregnancies are considered abortion. The health question that should be answered: is abortion medically necessary? Does it treat or solve any pregnancy-related complication that can't be addressed without aborting the unborn child?

Instead of addressing these relevant questions, the U.N. couched the women's health issue narrowly around the mother seeking a dangerous, illegal abortion.

And further stated the reason for making abortion illegal is the protection of the patriarchy introduced by European colonialism. Come on.

In researching this subject to form my opinion, I note that pro-abortion arguments are careful to use words like "fetus," "tissue," or "product of conception." Because, obviously, using the term "baby" humanizes it, and therefore aborting it might be akin to killing it. Dehumanizing it makes the act much more palatable.

In my home state of Pennsylvania, abortion is legal up until the 24th week. Thereafter, the mother must prove it is medically necessary for her health. I looked up a picture of a 23-week-old baby. I also viewed a step-by-step procedure depiction of a dilation and evacuation (D&E) abortion of a 23-week-old baby.

This is why, under the cloud of Roe v. Wade, anti-abortion legislatures in 27 states require ultra-sounds prior to an abortion. Skeptics think this is a veiled attempt to humanize the baby to the mother. I will go further to say it is definitely an attempt by the states that passed these laws to humanize the baby. If what is inside the mother is truly an inhuman fetus or tissue, then why do pro-abortion groups oppose these ultra-sound requirements?

Let both sides of this issue unveil their arguments. Pro-abortion – we know this is a baby, but because the consequence of carrying it falls primarily on the mother, having the choice to abort it is more important than the life of the baby. Anti-abortion – we know that we are forcing a woman to carry a baby that might relegate her to poverty or jeopardize her emotional well-being, but the unborn baby is not at fault and, therefore, should never be terminated.

I, on the other hand, am arguing balance. As I stated earlier in this chapter, I believe abortion kills babies. I'm confident that I am on the right side of this issue. But I'm not certain. If politicians and judges must decide, push this down to the states. Some states might be ultra-restrictive, and others might have little to no restrictions. Then, let people decide where they want to live (an ultra-restrictive or an ultra-permissive state).

My preference, in an ideal world, is abortions would diminish to near zero without laws or judicial decisions. Abortion would end because of our morality and humanity.

On Governance

I didn't read the full U.S. Constitution until I was 58 years old. My lack of curiosity astonished me since the "Constitution" is invoked over and over by those who might not have read it either. Many rely on my ignorance.

For example, did you know there is no separation between church and state in the Constitution? It only prohibits the federal government from creating a religion. Here is what the Constitution says in the First Amendment: "Congress shall make no law respecting an establishment of religion, or prohibiting the free exercise thereof."[49] More commonly phrased as the anti-establishment clause. In fact, one might legitimately argue that our zeal to purge religion from the public square is unconstitutional because of the "free exercise thereof" phrase. Not that I'm complaining. Rarely do people migrate to a theocracy.

The root source of federal law and the blueprint that compels us how to govern is the U.S. Constitution for all matters federal and state constitutions for all matters state. Laws enacted by the federal government must be within congressional powers granted by the Constitution and must not run afoul of it. For federal law, federal courts decide this if a branch of government runs roughshod over the Constitution.

Below the Constitution are myriads of laws that are permitted to be made within its framework, precedents set by courts in interpreting laws, particularly when they are not very specific and therefore challenged by citizens or groups (typically referred to as "case law"), and regulations enforced by unelected government employees to ensure those regulated obey the law. When I tried to look up how many U.S. laws there were, I couldn't find the answer. Let's just say there are a lot. And this is federal law. I'm not including state law or local ordinances.

In 2022, the Heritage Foundation, a conservative think-tank for sure, created an algorithm that scoured the United States Code, where federal laws are documented, and determined there were 5,199 federal crimes that we can commit as of 2019, a 36 percent increase since 1994. The study concluded[50]:

> *"These findings support the conclusion that the number of federal crimes has increased, while also bolstering concerns that federal crimes are too diffuse, too numerous, and too vague for the average citizen to know what the law requires."*

In 2011, civil rights attorney Harvey Silverglate wrote his book *Three Felonies a Day: How the Feds Target the Innocent*. The book describes how prosecutors can pin arguable federal crimes on any one of us for even the most seemingly innocuous behavior, such as: going abroad with too many pennies or nickels, punishable by up to five years in prison; engaging in weather modification behavior without first notifying the Secretary of Commerce or risk being fined up to $10,000; or using a falconry bird in a movie that is not about falconry. I'm not kidding. In this context, shouldn't we be glad that the rate of increase in law-making has recently gone down because Congress is so dysfunctional and can't get much accomplished?

True story: In 2019, a California man was detained for eating a sandwich at a public train station. Oddly, it is against California law to do so, punishable by up to a $250 fine and 48 hours of community service. I researched the video of the man being approached by police and the argument that ensued. My guess is the officer was on a fishing expedition looking for something much more substantial from the sandwich guy. The officer used an obscure law to detain someone with the hope that by doing so, he would find something more.

I realize we jailed Al Capone on tax evasion while suspecting he was guilty of things far worse. But is using our voluminous, hard-to-follow, and sometimes obscure federal, state, and local laws to single out people we don't like the society we want? This is where we are. By Silverglate's estimate, we commit three felonies per day. Which ones are you guilty of, and by whose grace are you not being prosecuted for them?

In addition to federal law, state law, local ordinances, and case law, U.S. citizens are subject to regulation that often goes beyond the law and is rife with unintended consequences. For example, in 2010, Congress passed the Dodd-Frank Act in reaction to the 2008 financial crisis. Section 1071 of that Act amended the Equal Credit Opportunity Act (ECOA) to require financial institutions to compile, maintain, and submit to the Consumer Finance Protection Bureau (CFPB) certain data on applications for credit for women-owned, minority-owned, and small businesses. In 2024, the CFPB finally issued its final ruling, and it was a doozy.

They required 81 data points to be reported, including, and in addition to race, gender, and sexual orientation, amount applied for versus amount approved, denial reason, pricing information, revenue of the applicant, ethnicity, and various other data points. You would have to be a fool to believe that the CFPB won't start firing off orders and press releases that this or that institution is racist or sexist because they turned down more applicants of [insert preferred classification here] than white guys. Their assertion won't be based on data controlled for things like traditional creditworthiness of the borrower. It rarely is. And we let them get away with it.

The rule required to be made by Section 1071 is being challenged in court by various trade associations because they know, as should we all, that this will result in the government picking which borrowers deserve credit from financial institutions, and creditworthiness will take a back seat. I have been in banking my entire career, outside of my military service, and have only witnessed bankers make credit decisions based on credit fundamentals that support the idea that the borrower will pay them back, regardless of race, gender, or sexual orientation. Financial institutions don't ask for that information for business loans as of this writing.

This is an example of how regulation plays a significant role in issues that affect us all—and it's mostly well-intentioned. We don't want credit decisions made based on race, gender, or sexual orientation. However, the CFPB rule implementing Dodd-Frank Section 1071 will do exactly that.

Bureaucracy

Why all this talk about federal, state, local, and case law and the resulting regulations in a discussion about governance? Because there are too many laws and regulations. The government is slowly inserting itself into everyone's everyday life—exactly what the founding fathers did not want.

There are occasions when administrative branches, such as the president or state governors, build discipline in the regulatory regime to reduce the burden on us. For example, in 2018, Jelena McWilliams became the chairwoman for the Federal Deposit Insurance Corporation (FDIC), a bank regulator that ensured the safety and soundness of our banking system and protected the FDIC insurance fund. When McWilliams took office, there were over 900 FDIC "guidance letters." Unlike a law or regulation, supervisory guidance does not have the force and effect of law.

As such, supervisory guidance does not create binding legal obligations. But that is not how "guidance" was enforced. So, McWilliams cut guidance letters almost in half.

Before she left in 2022, the FDIC issued a final rule on the role of supervisory guidance, reiterating the above, so that future bank guidance does not drift into obligatory regulation. There are not many Jelena McWilliams looking to deconstruct administrative authority through reduced regulation. Therefore, we must institutionalize it, similar to her parting shot on her final rule on the role of supervisory guidance.

In order to wind down the power unelected bureaucrats have over us, I propose that to enact one new regulation, two equal resource requirements must be abolished. Meaning, if a government agency proposes a new regulation that will require, say a restaurant to dedicate 100 hours per year to implement, then two regulations that require over 100 hours be abolished. If it requires four regulations to be abolished to exceed the 100 hours, so be it.

This will result in a downward trend in government interference in our free society, make it easier to do business in our free society, reduce the power of bureaucrats over us, and make regulation more effective because we will constantly be looking to abolish ineffective regulations to implement new and supposedly needed regulations. Wouldn't it make lawmakers who pass laws that lead to regulation and bureaucrats who propose regulation to follow the law think long and hard about how effective the regulation will be? They'll have to propose an offset to it. This is what committee hearings should be…

"The Chair recognizes the gentlewoman from Michigan."

"Thank you, Madame Chair. Sir (asking the Director of the Environmental Protection Agency), if we pass this law as proposed, how many regulatory compliance hours will we be adding to our utilities, what is the estimated cost and who will bear it, and what will be your proposed offset?"

Refreshing, right? We should demand better, more effective government.

New Laws

Turn on any news channel, left, right, center, and one common theme is that our federal government is not working. Any senator or representative can introduce a bill. But getting it to a vote seems nearly impossible, especially if the person introducing it is in the minority party.

Most bills die in a committee graveyard. If the proposer is in the minority party, the committee chair can simply not put it on the agenda. Or they can table it by deciding not to vote on it. If it doesn't make it out of committee, it doesn't go to the full House or Senate.

This nonsense is not in the Constitution. It is in rules made by the respective House or Senate. If rules inhibit the ability of representatives to bring bills for debate and vote, I'm at a loss as to why they are constitutional. Section 7 of the Constitution says nothing about killing a bill in committee. Minimally, each bill should be voted upon in committee, and if it passes out of committee by simple majority, it should be voted on by the full House or Senate. Even if not passed out of committee, there should be a relief valve under certain conditions to bring a bill to the floor so one committee member should not wield ungranted power to kill a bill.

Similar to the commonsense approach to reverse the advance of regulation, I propose limits for laws passed by Congress and signed into law by the President. If a law is passed, two similar consequential laws should be abolished. As I mentioned earlier, even if you thought you were law-abiding, there is not one person in the United States who knows this to be true. You likely commit crimes every day. Unpunished crimes…until someone has a reason to punish you.

No, we must make the laws and rules we must follow fewer and simpler. There is plenty of low-hanging fruit to implement this approach to reduce the number of laws we are subject to. It will force our legislative bodies to only pass laws that have the desired effect because they will need to find offsets to it. And if a law passes and doesn't meet the desired effect, then that law should be placed on the chopping block.

Which leads me to another point. The intention of a law should be clearly stated in its abstract. For example, if a law is passed designed to reduce the poverty rate, and within a reasonable time the poverty rate does not decline, the law sunsets and is no longer a law without any legislative action. This will reduce the incidence of ending a program where a beneficiary of the program gets on the local news and cries about why their children will suffer without it. Laws rarely die even if they fail at their intent, but if we implement this commonsense approach, they will.

Having a clear intent statement also helps regulators implement regulations to enforce the law, particularly if they have to fill in gaps due to a lack of clarity within the body of the law. It also gives the courts greater clarity in interpreting the law. If you submit a bill with the hope it turns into law yet can't give a clear intent statement, then I suggest not submitting it.

Budget Nonsense

The single greatest failing that falls on the shoulder of nearly every member of Congress at this writing is the over $35 trillion in debt they have rung up. The number keeps growing. This is partially our fault. I went to the ballot box and voted for my representative who never voted to reduce the deficit by my recollection. We praise Congress when they spend. We decry them when they cut. So, they stopped cutting. It's our mea culpa as well as theirs.

Since they have proven incapable of implementing fiscal discipline, it makes sense that we institutionalize it. This is how I propose we govern.

Demand our Congress to pass a law with the following points: Any representative or senator who votes to increase the budget deficit when the prior quarter's adjusted gross domestic product grows by greater than .5 percent annualized is ineligible for re-election unless the U.S. has declared a state of war. Place a limit on how much of an unpaid bill can be passed during times of recession. Emergency funding bills, or "continuing resolutions" count toward this objective so Congress can't play shenanigans to continue to spend unchecked using legal loopholes.

Any representative or senator who does not vote on an annual budget that reduces the deficit by at least ten percent or vote for a balanced budget if one exists prior to the fiscal year-end is ineligible for re-election. If there is a vote that does not pass, the representative or senator must vote and pass a budget within 30 calendar days of the prior budget not passing. If either the Senate or House of Representatives fails to do so, then all representatives and senators are ineligible for re-election.

Each of the House of Representatives and the Senate will undertake a review of its rules so this bill becomes an effective law to force members of Congress to systematically reduce the deficit until it is eliminated. To offset the ability of our representatives to use the 10% deficit reduction rule to run deficits well into the future, set a balanced budget end date such as 10 years.

The deficit has weakened us in terms of being the dominant economy in the world and sapped our resources needed to be the dominant military in the world that keeps despots at bay, and is saddling future generations with a level of debt that now equates to approximately $266,000 per household. Get out your checkbook; thank Congress in the memo line.

Conclusion

There you have it. Nine important issues that I researched, balancing the bias I found in my research while applying common sense, all of which helped me arrive at my opinion. Based on that same research, I don't expect you to come to the same conclusions. However, what I hope you get from reading this book is that you have the power at your fingertips to develop informed opinions so you can defend them with authority. What I also hope you get from reading this book is that you cannot rely on politicians, political actors (like action committees), or even biased media outlets to form your opinions.

A free and democratic society requires informed voters. Let us not be informed by sound bites, headlines, and political hacks. Let's instead rely on peer-reviewed research, news outlets deemed "unbiased" or "central," history, and our common sense. Research can empower us by providing the tools and information we need to participate meaningfully in democratic processes. When citizens are well-informed, they are more likely to engage in civic activities and hold their elected officials accountable. Isn't this a better result than finding our tribe on social media and yelling at the other side?

While social media can be a powerful tool for communication, awareness, and civic engagement, its potential for harm is undeniable and evident in our social streams. Turning this negative into a positive requires a combination of user knowledge, technological solutions, and, yes, some regulatory oversight. But not the censorship that we have seen.

In the introduction, I asserted that most readers want less poverty, less racism, and more economic mobility. Not all, though. Some thrive in the space of more poverty, more racism, and less economic mobility. And unfortunately, those in that camp have messages and slogans that fit neatly into sound bites and bullet points.

Let's go back to my opinion that it is not taxpayers' responsibility to feed other people's children. It is the parent's responsibility. But in a sound bite, "I fed the children" sounds great! Who would be against "feeding the children?"

What you won't find in a sound bite: I (meaning a politician, not to mention that it's taxpayer money) will feed the children, increasing parental dependence on me, and therefore, I will likely get those parents' votes. Do those parents want to be dependent on the government? Probably not. But it certainly saps their resolve to improve their situation so they don't rely on the government to feed their children. Like I said, most want less poverty. Not all.

Aside from Charlie Munger–like cynicism, I am optimistic about our future. People still want to come here, people don't want to leave here, other countries still buy our debt, and power here is distributed more widely than in most other countries.

Our future is dependent on us. Democracy works in sunlight where accountability is strong, power is distributed, and freedom is real. When we are free to pursue what is in our best interests, the economy grows, all income levels lives improve, and the government is not involved in any significant way in our everyday lives.

Don't take my word for it. Look it up from reliable, minimally biased sources, and apply some good old common sense.

Democracy is delicate. Let us be its guardians.

Endnotes

1 2023, September 19. Views on US political system, trust in government, federal-state relations | Pew Research Center. https://www.pewresearch.org/politics/2023/09/19/views-of-the-u-s-political-system-the-federal-government-and-federal-state-relations/

2 Moranto, R. 2023, September 2. I'm a conservative. Is there still a place for me in the field of political science? (thehill.com). https://thehill.com/opinion/education/4180961-im-a-conservative-is-there-still-a-place-for-me-in-the-field-of-political-science/

3 2024. Media Bias Chart | AllSides. https://www.allsides.com/media-bias/media-bias-chart

4 Ardrey, T. 2022, August 14. Presidential historian says he's never seen a former president 'take ultra-classified documents, stick them in his basement' (yahoo.com). Business Insider. https://www.yahoo.com/news/presidential-historian-says-hes-never-195335741.html

5 Mangan, D, Kinery, E. 2023, January 12. President Biden had classified documents in Delaware garage (cnbc.com). https://www.cnbc.com/2023/01/12/president-biden-had-classified-documents-in-delaware-garage.html

6 Konen, J. 2021, June 30. Do Teachers Get Good Benefits? | Health Insurance, Salary | Teacher.org. https://www.teacher.org/blog/ever-wonder-what-your-teacher-benefits-are-really-worth/

7 2023. Expenditures for public elementary and secondary education and other related programs, by function: Selected school years,

1919-20 through 2020-21. National Center for Education Statistics. https://nces.ed.gov/programs/digest/d23/tables/dt23_236.10.asp

8 Loeb, S. 2016, January 14. Half the people working in schools aren't classroom teachers—so what? | Brookings. https://www.brookings.edu/articles/half-the-people-working-in-schools-arent-classroom-teachers-so-what/

9 Richmond, M. 2014, August. The Hidden Half: School Employees Who Don't Teach. Thomas B. Fordham Institute, https://files.eric.ed.gov/fulltext/ED560006.pdf

10 Pierce, E, Claybourn, C. 2023, August 29. Private School vs. Public School (usnews.com). https://www.usnews.com/education/k12/articles/private-school-vs-public-school

11 Schaeffer, K. 2022, April 12, 10 facts about U.S. college graduates | Pew Research Center. https://www.pewresearch.org/short-reads/2022/04/12/10-facts-about-todays-college-graduates/

12 Jones Jr., L. 2023, June 1. One Culprit in Rising College Costs: Administrative Expenses | Education | U.S. News (usnews.com). https://www.usnews.com/education/articles/one-culprit-in-rising-college-costs

13 Terrell, K. 2022, December 27. The Top 20 Jobs That Will Be in Demand in 2023 (aarp.org). https://www.aarp.org/work/job-search/in-demand-jobs-2023/

14 Lazear, E. 2020. Socialism, Capitalism and Income. Hoover Institution. prosperityproject_lazear_final.pdf (hoover.org).

15 Munger, C. 2022, February 20. Charlie Munger: Envy, Not Greed, That Runs (Ruins) The World | Ep. 1_【ENG CC SUB】_(youtube.com). https://youtu.be/20M26u0kFzE?si=bNew0Mf024-fS5u9

16 Undated. Become a Teacher in Pennsylvania. Teach.com. https://teach.com/careers/become-a-teacher/teaching-credential/state-requirements/pennsylvania/

17 2024. US Education Statistics and Data Trends: public school spending, educational attainment, and more | USAFacts. https://usafacts.org/topics/education/#f2dedd35-afb1-4efb-aa65-059f6ee66d3d

18 Jameel, M, Shapiro, L, Yerardi, J. 2019, February 28. The numbers behind workplace discrimination - Washington Post. https://www.washingtonpost.com/graphics/2019/business/discrimination-complaint-outcomes/

19 Davis Jr., E. 2024, February 21. 10 Countries That Take the Most Immigrants | Best Countries | U.S. News (usnews.com). https://www.usnews.com/news/best-countries/slideshows/10-countries-that-take-the-most-immigrants?slide=11

20 Supreme Court of the United States. 2010, January 21. 08-205 Citizens United v. Federal Election Comm'n (01/21/10) (fec.gov). https://www.fec.gov/resources/legal-resources/litigation/cu_sc08_opinion.pdf

21 Kim, A. 2022, July 13. Maryland is latest test of Dem efforts to sway GOP primaries and focus on conservative picks - ABC News. https://abcnews.go.com/Politics/maryland-latest-test-dem-efforts-sway-gop-primaries/story?id=86617925

22 Omatz, M. 2022, August 18. Republicans Turn Against the League of Women Voters — ProPublica. https://www.propublica.org/article/league-of-women-voters-gop-trump

23 2018, August 13. Chinese state media defends crackdown on Muslim Uighurs – DW – 08/13/2018. https://www.dw.com/en/china-

state-media-justify-muslim-uighur-crackdown-to-prevent-chinas-syria/a-45055678

24 2024. Media Bias Chart | AllSides. https://www.allsides.com/media-bias/media-bias-chart

25 Krieg, G. 2018, November 17. Stacey Abrams says 'democracy failed' Georgia as she ends bid for governor | CNN Politics. https://www.cnn.com/2018/11/16/politics/stacey-abrams-concession/index.html

26 Marquardt, A. 2020, November 13. Federal election official blasts Trump's false election claims as 'laughable,' 'baffling' and 'insulting' | CNN Politics. https://www.cnn.com/2020/11/13/politics/hovland-trump-election-claims/index.html

27 2022, August 18. Watch: Young boy rushes up to the Pope. See what happens next | CNN. https://www.cnn.com/videos/world/2022/08/18/boy-joins-pope-francis-in-service-mxp-vpx.hln

28 2014, September 6. SPJ Code of Ethics - Society of Professional Journalists. https://www.spj.org/ethicscode.asp

29 Cusick, M. 2019, March 28. 40 Years After Nation's Worst Nuclear Accident, A Push To Keep Three Mile Island : NPR. https://www.npr.org/2019/03/28/707000226/40-years-after-a-partial-nuclear-meltdown-a-new-push-to-keep-three-mile-island-o

30 Simon, J. 2022, August 31. Sharing news you didn't read can feel like expertise - Futurity. https://www.futurity.org/sharing-news-expert-2792872-2/

31 Cronin, J. Undated. UK Healthcare System: What Foreigners Need to Know (internationalinsurance.com). International Citizens Insurance. https://www.internationalinsurance.com/health/systems/uk.php

32 Blake, I. 2021, April 15. One in four people waiting over four months for their heart surgery and other heart procedures (bhf.org.uk). British Heart Foundation. https://www.bhf.org.uk/what-we-do/news-from-the-bhf/news-archive/2021/april/more-heart-patients-waiting-over-year-surgery-procedures

33 Marshall, E, Miller, L, Moritz, L. 2023, July 6. Challenges and impacts from wait times for specialist care identified by primary care providers: Results from the MAAP study cross-sectional survey - PMC (nih.gov). National Institute for Health. https://pmc.ncbi.nlm.nih.gov/articles/PMC10448708/

34 Undated. Best Healthcare in the World 2022 (worldpopulationreview.com). World Population Review of CEOWorld Magazine data. https://worldpopulationreview.com/country-rankings/best-healthcare-in-the-world

35 Himmelstein, D, Campbell, T, Woolhandler, S. 2020, January 7. Health Care Administrative Costs in the United States and Canada, 2017 | Annals of Internal Medicine (acpjournals.org). https://www.acpjournals.org/doi/10.7326/M19-2818

36 Coughlin, T, Samuel-Jakobos, H, Garfield, R. 2021, April. Sources of Payment of Uncompensated Care for the Uninsured. Urban.org. https://www.urban.org/sites/default/files/publication/104173/sources-of-payment-for-uncompensated-care-for-the-uninsured.pdf

37 Vermeer, T, Durante, A, York, E, Walczak, J. 2023, March 30. Who Pays Taxes: Federal State Local Tax Burden, Government Transfers (taxfoundation.org). https://taxfoundation.org/research/all/federal/who-pays-taxes-federal-state-local-tax-burden-transfers/

38 Lawder, D. 2023, October 20. US budget gap soars to $1.7 trillion, largest outside COVID era | Reuters. https://www.reuters.com/

world/us/us-budget-deficit-jumps-23-nearly-17-trillion-social-security-health-costs-rise-2023-10-20/

39 2024. Reelection Rates Over the Years • OpenSecrets. https://www.opensecrets.org/elections-overview/reelection-rates

40 Barrow, R. de Rugy, V. 2013, May 7. Defense Spending and the Economy | Mercatus Center. https://www.mercatus.org/research/research-papers/defense-spending-and-economy

41 The White House. 2022, March. Governmental Receipts (whitehouse.gov). https://www.whitehouse.gov/wp-content/uploads/2022/03/ap_11_receipts_fy2023.pdf

42 Associated Press. 2023, October 13. Gap between U.S. income taxes owed and paid is set to keep growing, IRS says : NPR. https://www.npr.org/2023/10/13/1205663467/income-tax-gap-keep-growing?sc=18&f=1001

43 Friedman, J. 2016, March 11. The IRS Attacks the Tea Party -Capital Research Center. https://capitalresearch.org/article/irs_tea_party/

44 Bernard, K, Gutierrez, L. 2022, August 5. Kansas rejects abortion amendment: 2022 election vote results | The Kansas City Star. https://www.kansascity.com/news/politics-government/election/article263832087.html

45 Gaitan, E, Steupert, M, Cox, T. 2024, May 24. Fact Sheet: Reasons for Abortion - Charlotte Lozier Institute. https://lozierinstitute.org/fact-sheet-reasons-for-abortion/#_edn3

46 ABC News. 2006, April 14. Does Abortion Lower Crime Rates? - ABC News (go.com). https://abcnews.go.com/2020/story?id=1843646&page=1

47 National Right to Life Committee. 2018, April 2. State Homicide Laws That Recognize Unborn Victims | National Right to Life (nrlc.org). https://nrlc.org/federal/unbornvictims/statehomicidelaws092302/

48 United Nations Office of the High Commissioner. 2021, September 28. Abortion is essential healthcare and women's health must be prioritized over politics | OHCHR. https://www.ohchr.org/en/statements/2021/09/abortion-essential-healthcare-and-womens-health-must-be-prioritized-over

49 U.S. Constitution | Constitution Annotated | Congress.gov | Library of Congress. https://constitution.congress.gov/constitution/

50 Canaparo, G, McLaughlin, P, Nelson, J, Palagashvili, L. 2022, January 7. Count the Code: Quantifying Federalization of Criminal Statutes | The Heritage Foundation. https://www.heritage.org/crime-and-justice/report/count-the-code-quantifying-federalization-criminal-statutes

Made in United States
Troutdale, OR
11/03/2026

56844424R00060